Create Great iPhone Photos

Create Great iPhone Photos

Apps, Tips, Tricks, and Effects

ALLAN HOFFMAN

Create Great iPhone Photos. Copyright © 2011 by Allan Hoffman

15 14 13 12 11   1 2 3 4 5 6 7 8 9

ISBN-10: 1-59327-285-5
ISBN-13: 978-1-59327-285-2

Publisher: William Pollock
Production Editor: Serena Yang
Cover and Interior Design: Octopod Studios
Developmental Editor: Tyler Ortman
Copyeditor: Kim Wimpsett
Compositors: Riley Hoffman and Alison Law
Proofreader: Ward Webber
Indexer: Valerie Haynes Perry

For information on book distributors or translations, please contact No Starch Press, Inc. directly:

No Starch Press, Inc.
38 Ringold Street, San Francisco, CA 94103
phone: 415.863.9900; fax: 415.863.9950; info@nostarch.com; http://www.nostarch.com/

Library of Congress Cataloging-in-Publication Data

Hoffman, Allan, 1962-
 Create great iPhone photos : apps, tips, tricks, and effects / by Allan Hoffman.
      p. cm.
 Includes bibliographical references and index.
 ISBN-13: 978-1-59327-285-2
 ISBN-10: 1-59327-285-5
 1. Photography--Amateurs' manuals. 2. iPhone (Smartphone)--Amateurs' manuals. I. Title.
 TR146.H66 2011
 770.285--dc22
                                    2010045899

Printed in Canada

Dedication

For Dianne

Acknowledgments

So many people helped transform this from an idea into a book. Thanks to Bill Pollock, the publisher of No Starch Press, for going for the idea, and to my editor, Tyler Ortman, for his commitment to the book and keen advice and guidance along the way. Thanks to the entire No Starch Press crew for their creativity and dedication to the craft of book publishing. Special thanks to my parents for buying me that Konica T-4 back in 1978 and to my dad for keeping assorted photographic gadgetry around the house and inspiring me with his own love of photography. Much appreciation and love to my wife, Dianne Rosky, for her advice, enthusiasm, and steadfast support, and to our kids, Ruby and Levi, for making everything worth it. Thanks to my brother, Dan, for the geeky conversation and creative ideas. Mark Aldrin Bantigue, Sean Kaufman, and Jessica Romero provided creative and organizational support along the way. iPhone photography wouldn't even exist except for the innovators behind apps like TiltShift Generator, PictureShow, Hipstamatic, and scores of others.

Brief Contents

Contents in Detail

Introduction

As everyone knows, the iPhone is far more than a phone. It's an e-book reader, a gaming device, a music player, and even a tool for banking and blogging. And it's a camera, too—a rather extraordinary one. Millions now use the iPhone camera as their camera of choice, snapping images of their buddies' hijinks, their kids' birthdays, and just about anything else crossing their line of vision. But it's one thing to use the iPhone for occasional snapshots and another to explore the wondrous possibilities of iPhone photography. Yes, camera phones are everywhere, but the iPhone camera is in a class of its own, largely because of the innovative and breathtakingly varied photography apps available for it. With these apps, you're able to transform your iPhone camera into a fun and inspirational tool for photographic creativity. This book tells you how.

The fans of iPhone photography are a varied bunch, from casual photographers experimenting with photo booth apps to teenagers documenting their lives with the camera in their pockets. Even professional photographers have become obsessed with the iPhone camera, wowed by its ability to replicate effects and techniques previously requiring costly gear, a photo studio, and a digital darkroom. This book is for anyone with an iPhone camera who's looking for advice, tips, and tools to make the most of the iPhone's camera and its photographic capabilities. You have an iPhone? You use its camera? Then this book is for you. It'll give you straightforward, accessible how-to advice to help you take awesome iPhone photos.

iPhone Basics

This book assumes you've already fooled around with your iPhone and learned how it works. In particular, it assumes you know how to perform essential operations with your iPhone, such as tapping the iPhone screen to open an app. (For complete newbies, a free iPhone manual is available at *http://www.apple.com/ support/iphone/.*) Of course, even if you know how to use your iPhone, you may not be familiar with the terminology for every aspect of the iPhone's Multi-Touch interface. These terms and techniques, in particular, may come in handy when reading this book and learning about iPhone photography:

▶ **Flick**   By flicking a finger across your screen, you're able to move from one image to another in many apps, such as the iPhone's built-in Photos app.

▶ **Double-tap**   To inspect image details by zooming, you're often able to double-tap the spot where you want to zoom in. Double-tap again to zoom out.

▶ **Pinch-and-spread**   You have more control when zooming with the so-called pinch-and-spread technique. By touching the screen with two fingers, typically your thumb and forefinger, you're able to "pinch" those fingers together to zoom in on an image. Spread your fingers apart to zoom out.

▶ **Touch and hold**   To drag an image around the screen, touch your finger to the screen, and then hold it there for a moment.

▶ **Shutter button (📷)**   This is how you'll take pictures using the iPhone's Camera app.

▶ **Action icon (📤)**   The action icon is used to perform actions like emailing, saving, or texting a photo.

▶ **Home screens**   Apple refers to the multiple screens on your iPhone, filled with apps, as Home screens. You can always get to your Home screens by pressing the Home button.

Much of the material in this book will apply no matter what model iPhone you're using or what version of the iPhone operating system you have installed on your iPhone. For consistency, I assume you're using iOS 4. And although I assume you're using an iPhone, many of the apps and techniques discussed here will also work just fine with an iPod touch.

What This Book Covers

You can do amazing things with your iPhone camera. You can add a lovely background blur to a photo, snap a photo with the look of a Polaroid from the 1970s, create black-and-white photo booth strips, and even post right to your photoblog, just seconds after snapping an image. All of this is possible with your iPhone, and this book will help you do it. Here's a quick rundown of the chapters:

In **Chapter 1: iPhone Camera Essentials**, you'll learn how to use your iPhone camera, view and share photos, and transfer photos between your iPhone and your computer. Topics include the iPhone's tap-to-focus system, zoom and macro capabilities, HDR options, slide shows, and accessories.

Chapter 2: Customize Your iPhone Camera explains how to add features to your iPhone, such as burst mode, a self-timer, and lots more. You'll learn how to find and install photography apps, including apps to replace the standard Camera app.

Chapter 3: Photoshop in Your Pocket has tutorials and guidance on using powerful image editors to crop images, retouch your photos, and fine-tune them by adjusting the color, contrast, exposure, and saturation. You'll learn how to use levels, layers, and curves for complex effects with apps like Photoshop Express, Photogene, PhotoForge, and Iris Photo Suite.

In **Chapter 4: Filters, Effects, and Recipes**, you'll learn about tools to transform your images with sophisticated combinations of filters and effects. You'll create background blurs, fake-miniature images, panoramas, double exposures, and unique frames with apps like Photo fx, TiltShift Generator, and AutoStitch Panorama.

Chapter 5: The Retro Look shows you how to reproduce the look of images from cameras, photographic films, and darkroom processes of yesteryear. You'll experiment with camera apps devoted to a vintage look, such as Hipstamatic, Lo-Mob, and ShakeItPhoto, and use apps that re-create the darkroom experience.

In **Chapter 6: Fun and Offbeat Effects**, you'll amuse yourself with apps to create photo booth strips, produce photos out of LEGO blocks, transform snapshots into Picasso paintings and psychedelic art, combine multiple images in a single frame, and produce comic strips and graphic novel sketches. You'll also learn to use apps to produce the beautiful mistakes from plastic toy cameras.

Chapter 7: Snap—and Share and **Chapter 8: Your Photoblog** show you how to become part of the photography community. You'll learn about apps to post images to the Flickr photo-sharing website, as well as to Twitter and Facebook, and explore options for sharing photos with the iPhone's location-detection capabilities. Then you'll learn how to create a photoblog with tools such as Tumblr, WordPress, Posterous, and Blogger.

Chapter 9: For Inspiration gives you photographs, advice, and favorite apps from leading iPhone photographers.

Where should you start? If you're new to iPhone photography, then the first two chapters provide a friendly, no-nonsense introduction to everything from the iPhone's sophisticated focus and exposure controls to the tools available to transform your iPhone into your dream camera. (Even experienced iPhone photographers will likely glean tips from the material in these chapters.) The remaining chapters explore the tips, tricks, effects, and—let's face it—pure photographic fun you can have with your iPhone. These chapters build on each other, but feel free to skip among them for the information that's of most interest to you.

1 iPhone Camera Essentials

Using the iPhone camera couldn't be simpler. Tap the screen, and presto, you've got your photo. That's all there is to it, right? Well, not exactly. As it turns out, the iPhone camera is deceptive in its simplicity.

Think of your iPhone camera as a blank slate, just waiting for you to transform it into the most amazing camera you've ever owned—an inspiring tool for photographic experimentation and creativity. With the help of an innovative ecosystem of photography apps, you're able to convert the iPhone's bare-bones camera into a magical camera-and-darkroom combo. Soon enough, your iPhone camera will be as feature-filled as a digital single-lens reflex (SLR)—and far more fun and versatile. One minute you'll be capturing photos with the hipster look of the Lomo LC-A camera, and the next you'll be snapping a series of images for an arcade photo booth strip.

Before you know it, you may realize your Canon or Nikon is snug in its case and your iPhone is now your de facto camera of choice. If you're looking to explore the boundaries of photographic creativity, there's no better way than with the iPhone.

Reasons to Love Your iPhone Camera

I've been obsessed with photography since I was a teenager. I got an SLR when I was 15 and proceeded to spend an absurd amount of time watching the silver drift off photographic paper in my high school's darkroom. I loved it—the amber glow of the darkroom light, the acrid odor of the fixer, the sheer magic of images appearing from nowhere.

Yet I've never had as much fun with photography as I have with my iPhone camera. Here's why:

▶ **It's always with you.** The iPhone camera encourages spontaneity and experimentation (see Figure 1-1). It's slim, it's lightweight, and it's always with you. You can slip the iPhone camera out of your purse or pocket and grab a shot.

▶ **You can customize the camera.** Other cameras have a fixed set of features. Not the iPhone. Any number of apps let you customize the camera with features such as a self-timer and burst mode.

▶ **You have Photoshop in your pocket.** By focusing on discrete tasks, the iPhone's photography apps make Photoshop-like effects relatively easy to accomplish, without the hassles (and learning curve) of Photoshop's menus and palettes. Just tap an app, and seconds later—right on your iPhone!— you're altering the image's color saturation or reproducing the look of a Polaroid SX-70 camera.

FIGURE 1-1: *iPhone photography doesn't require a lot of planning. See something interesting? Grab a shot.*

▶ **Snap, tweak, publish.** Nothing compares to the ease of taking a photo with the iPhone, creating a luscious blur or applying an off-the-wall filter, and then publishing it to your photoblog (see Figure 1-2). You're liberated from connection cables and hard-to-master photo-editing tools.

FIGURE 1-2: This image was captured, tweaked in TiltShift Generator, and posted to my photoblog on a train into New York City, all within about a minute.

Like lots of other people, I started using my iPhone camera out of convenience, and my initial forays were typical cell phone fare: my kids being silly or a chair I thought my wife might like in our living room. Then, after seeing the images it could produce—and exploring the ingenious (and, frankly, addictive) apps for editing them—I realized the iPhone camera was far more than a toy. There's something wonderfully visceral, even intimate, about iPhone photography, akin to the raw physicality of working with chemicals and photographic paper in a darkroom. As with so much about the iPhone, it's all about the touch interface—your ability to touch your photos and to enhance and manipulate them as your fingers glide over the iPhone's glass screen. Even professional photographers, who are used to lugging around heavy SLRs, hulking lenses, and elaborate lighting contraptions, have become infatuated with iPhone photography. Chase Jarvis, whose clients include Nikon and Reebok, published a book of his iPhone images: *The Best Camera Is the One That's With You* (New Riders Press, 2009). As he says in the book, "As an artist, I feel more free with the little camera built into my iPhone than I ever have with any other camera." Associated Press photographer David Guttenfelder, a finalist for the Pulitzer Prize, used his iPhone camera to capture images of Marines during the Marjah offensive in Afghanistan. You might be entirely new to photography and view the iPhone as a way to learn and experiment, or you might be an experienced photographer who sees it as just another tool—a surprisingly versatile one—in your photographic arsenal. Whatever the case, you'll likely learn to love the iPhone camera.

Simplicity—and Limitations

Compared to many digital cameras, the iPhone camera is lacking in terms of megapixels and manual controls. Yet for many photographers, including professionals, the joys of iPhone photography are inextricably intertwined with those limitations. Other cameras, even ones meant for the tech-averse, typically have an assortment of buttons and dials to choose scene modes, adjust the exposure, and view the results. With iPhone photography, the focus is, quite literally, on the image. There's something pure and liberating about its simplicity.

But the limitations are real, and knowing them can help you know what to expect from your iPhone camera:

FIGURE 1-3: *Embrace the iPhone's limitations. Sometimes the lack of control over the shutter speed produces an appealing, if unintended, blur.*

▶ **You're not able to control the shutter speed.** Cameras with manual controls (or special "scene" settings) let you determine whether you want a fast shutter speed—1/1000th of a second, say—to stop the action. With the iPhone, the shutter speed is set based on the lighting conditions. If you've got a moving subject, like a three-year-old kid who won't sit still or a player in a sporting event, you shouldn't depend on your iPhone camera. Although you can shoot action shots, they'll often be blurry (see Figure 1-3).

▶ **The aperture is fixed.** In tandem with the shutter speed, the *aperture*, or lens opening, determines how much light reaches your camera's sensor. The aperture is fixed at *f*/2.4 for the iPhone 4 and *f*/2.8 for other iPhone models.

▶ **There is no traditional flash.** The iPhone 4's flash is LED-based and underpowered compared to traditional flashes. The earlier iPhone models have no flash. Because of this, photos taken under low-light conditions may have a grainy appearance (with a lot of *noise*, in the parlance of digital photography), especially if you attempt to print them (see Figure 1-4).

▶ **Don't expect to print big.** The iPhone's photos just aren't meant for poster-sized prints.

FIGURE 1-4: *Noise is visible in areas of this image from an iPhone 4, especially when enlarged, but it's an improvement from earlier models.*

Is the iPhone camera suitable for every occasion? In a word, no. You're going on a safari? Bring a camera with a high-powered zoom lens. Knowing the iPhone's limitations will help you know when to opt for your iPhone camera and when not to.

  # The iPhone's Duo of Photography Apps

Two photography apps work in tandem to help you take photographs and then view them: the Camera app and the Photos app.

With these apps, you can snap images, store them, and share photos with friends by email or online. As you learn more about iPhone photography, you may find yourself choosing other apps for these tasks (yes, it's possible to use other apps to take photos with the iPhone camera), but chances are the Camera and Photos apps will still be mainstays of your iPhone photography experience.

Taking Photos with the Camera App

Here's how you take a photo with your iPhone:

1. Tap the **Camera** app.
2. Compose your image. The iPhone screen serves as a big, bright viewfinder. The world looks great on it.
3. Tap the button, as shown in Figure 1-5. If you don't have your iPhone in silent mode, you'll hear a lovely shutter sound, just as if you were taking the photo with a 1960s-era SLR.
4. As the image is captured, you will see a shutter close over the image, and your photo will zip into the Camera Roll.
5. Now you're ready to take another.

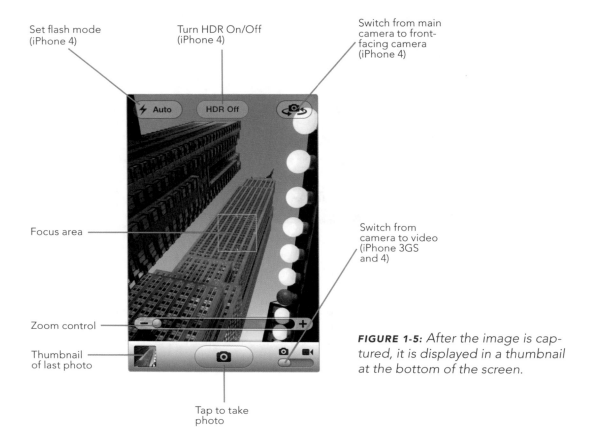

Set flash mode
(iPhone 4)

Turn HDR On/Off
(iPhone 4)

Switch from main
camera to front-
facing camera
(iPhone 4)

Focus area

Switch from
camera to video
(iPhone 3GS
and 4)

Zoom control

Thumbnail
of last photo

FIGURE 1-5: *After the image is cap-tured, it is displayed in a thumbnail at the bottom of the screen.*

Tap to take
photo

Awesome, you've got a photo. Simple as could be. Can things go awry? Surely. Here are a few hints to help ensure you're not bungling this:

▶ **Don't block the lens.**   The camera lens isn't a prominent feature of the iPhone. It's a smallish hole at the top-left corner on the back of the iPhone. Your finger may occasionally stray in front of it. Get away, finger.

▶ **Press; then release.**   The iPhone doesn't actually capture a photo until you remove your finger from the 📷 button. Avoid giving the button a hard tap—a surefire way to jolt the iPhone and get a blurry image. Instead, hold your finger to the 📷 button as you compose your shot, ensure the camera is steady, and then release.

▶ **Keep the lens clean.**   Dust on the lens can mar your photos. Use a micro-fiber lens-cleaning cloth, available at many camera stores, to keep the lens clean.

The Evolution of the iPhone Camera

Apple made major improvements to the iPhone camera with both the iPhone 4 and the iPhone 3GS. Both cameras produce significantly better images than the original iPhone and the iPhone 3G, especially in low-light conditions. Still, the iPhone isn't about to win a contest when it comes to megapixels, which is the spec many people use as a shortcut to evaluate camera quality. Even the iPhone 4's megapixels fall short of what's available in today's point-and-shoot digital cameras, many of them boasting 10-megapixel sensors. Megapixels matter, yet probably not as much as you think. The reason? Photographic quality depends on a variety of factors, such as the camera's lens, the size of its image sensor, the size of the pixels on the sensor, and a host of other complex technical details related to the way the sensor records light. The iPhone may not be a winner in terms of megapixels, but it is widely viewed as being capable of producing gorgeous images. Table 1-1 gives a rundown of the four iPhone models and the specs of their cameras.

Table 1-1: Comparison of iPhone Cameras

	iPhone 4	iPhone 3GS	iPhone 3G	iPhone
Megapixels	5 megapixels	3 megapixels	2 megapixels	2 megapixels
Photo resolution	2592 × 1936	2048 × 1536	1600 × 1200	1600 × 1200
Focus	Autofocus	Autofocus	Fixed focus	Fixed focus
Tap-to-focus	Yes	Yes	No	No
Video	HD (720p)	VGA	No	No
Geotagging	Yes	Yes	Yes	Yes
White balance	Yes	Yes	No	No
Macro	Yes	Yes	No	No
Front-facing camera	Yes	No	No	No
Flash	Yes	No	No	No
Aperture	f/2.4	f/2.8	f/2.8	f/2.8
Focal length	3.85 mm	3.85 mm	3.85 mm	3.85 mm

The iPhone 4 camera, in particular, captures photos approaching the quality of those from point-and-shoot digital cameras. We have the iPhone 4's image sensor to thank for this. The iPhone 4 uses a special type of sensor, with a technique known as *backside illumination*, to increase the sensor's light sensitivity in comparison to earlier iPhone models. The backside illumination technology allows Apple to include a small sensor, of the type needed for a phone, yet also increase the quality of iPhone images taken in low-light conditions. Compared to other iPhone models, the iPhone 4 produces images with a wider field of view, resulting in wider-angle photos. (The *field of view* is the photographic term for the area of a scene captured by your camera.)

Focus, Exposure, and White Balance (iPhone 3GS and iPhone 4)

The iPhone 3GS introduced a much-loved feature of the iPhone camera, known as *tap to focus*—the ability to tap your iPhone screen as a way to selectively auto-focus anywhere in the camera frame. That gives you a lot more control, and it makes the iPhone a far more capable camera. Here's how it works:

1. Whenever you're using the Camera app, a white square appears in the center of the display, which indicates where the camera will focus.
2. After the camera focuses, this white box disappears.
3. To adjust the focus, just tap somewhere else on the screen, as in Figure 1-6. The iPhone camera will shift the focus to the spot you tapped.

Where the Camera app automatically focused

Focus shifted by tapping this spot on the iPhone screen

FIGURE 1-6: *By tapping different spots on the iPhone screen, you can change the focus within the frame.*

In fact, the iPhone's tap-to-focus mechanism adjusts more than the focus. It also adjusts the exposure and white balance:

▶ **Exposure** Tap the screen, and the iPhone will adjust the *exposure*—the amount of light reaching the iPhone's image sensor—for that spot. So if there's a too-dark, underexposed area of the image (or, conversely, a bright, overexposed area), you can adjust the exposure for that spot by tapping that portion of the photo; the exposure of your image will be adjusted accordingly, as in Figure 1-7.

Exposure adjusted by
tapping this spot

Exposure adjusted by
tapping this spot

FIGURE 1-7: *By tapping different areas of the image, you can play with the exposure and achieve a variety of results.*

▶ **White balance** Adjustments to the *white balance*—the overall color temperature of an image—determine how realistic colors appear in a scene. If the colors seem "off" on the iPhone's screen, try tapping the square focus box to another spot; the adjustment in the white balance may improve the image (though you may have better luck by adjusting this with a photography app after you've captured the image).

The feature seems simple, but it's powerful: It essentially gives the iPhone something like spot metering capabilities—the ability to adjust the exposure based on the light readings in a fraction of the frame. With a traditional camera with manual controls, you often need to know the ins and outs of aperture controls and f-stops to make sophisticated adjustments to exposure; and even if you know all about this, there's a fair amount of guesswork. Yet with the iPhone, adjusting the exposure to get the desired results is blissfully intuitive. You tap the area of the image you want exposed correctly, and the exposure is adjusted.

To see for yourself, try this experiment:

1. On a sunny day, position a person (or an object, if you don't have a willing model) with his back to the sun. Take one photo without any adjustments.

2. Without moving the camera position, adjust the exposure by tapping the person or object, which should be in a shadow area of the frame. Next, snap your photo.

3. Compare the two images. You should see a notable difference, with the latter shot bringing out the highlights in your subject.

Zoom

What sort of camera doesn't have a zoom these days? Apple finally added zoom capabilities to the iPhone camera in the iOS 4 operating system. Alas, the iPhone's 5X zoom feature isn't an actual zoom lens, like those in point-and-shoot cameras; it is what is known as a *digital zoom*: The iPhone's technical wizardry, rather than the lens, simulates a zoom. Images from the zoom have the same resolution as any other image, yet there's a decrease in image quality because of the interpolation required to create the zoom effect (as shown in Figure 1-8). Don't overdo it with the zoom lens, because your image quality will suffer.

FIGURE 1-8: *Image quality declines when you use the zoom.*

Here's how to use the zoom:

1. Tap the **Camera** app.
2. Tap the screen. The zoom slider appears.
3. Glide your finger along the slider to zoom in and zoom out, as shown in Figure 1-9.

FIGURE 1-9: *The zoom slider lets you fill the frame with faraway objects or scenery. When composing an image with the zoom, the scene may appear somewhat blurry.*

Macro (iPhone 3GS and iPhone 4)

The latest iPhone models include a *macro* feature that lets you take close-ups with the camera. Simply tap the area you want to be in focus, and you'll be able to snap in-focus images as close as 3 to 4 inches from the camera lens (Figure 1-10).

FIGURE 1-10: *With the iPhone's macro lens, your subject will stay in focus as close as about 3 to 4 inches.*

HDR (iPhone 4)

High dynamic range (HDR) photography is a technique for capturing the light and dark areas of a scene in one image, typically by combining multiple images. By blending images in this way, the iPhone is able to capture details throughout the image, as if every area of the image were exposed properly—or so one hopes. HDR is something of an art, and your results will vary, especially since you're using the iPhone camera, which is not exactly designed for HDR.

Here's how to capture an HDR image with the iPhone's Camera app:

1. Tap the iPhone's **Settings** app, and then select **Photos**. Under HDR, switch Keep Normal Photo to **On**, which will preserve your original image in addition to the HDR image.
2. From the Camera app, tap the **HDR Off** button (as shown in Figure 1-5) to switch from HDR Off to HDR On.
3. Steady your camera, and then tap 📷 to take your photo. The iPhone takes three images and blends the best parts of them to create the HDR image.

Apple's version of HDR is quite subtle. If you're looking for an HDR app with the sort of eye-popping results often associated with HDR imagery, consider Pro HDR (see Chapter 4).

Flash (iPhone 4)

The iPhone 4 includes an LED flash, which means you actually have a way to capture iPhone images when you're in a dark cave or a dim nightclub. (Of course, if you want to capture an image discreetly, make sure you have the flash turned to Off!) The flash produces a blast of white light, and it's more than adequate to light up friends or family. However, the results can be mixed; it's certainly not always what you'd call a natural look. You'll want to use the iPhone flash selectively, and to do that, you need to know how to operate it, as shown in Figure 1-11:

FIGURE 1-11: *The iPhone 4 flash has three settings*

▶ **Flash controls** From the Camera app, tap the **Auto** button to open the flash controls. Your screen will display whatever option is selected: Off, Auto, or On. To revert to previous controls, tap the option that's displayed.

▶ **Auto** By default, the flash is set to fire automatically in dim and dark lighting conditions.

▶ **Off** Tap **Off** to ensure the iPhone flash doesn't fire—no matter how dark it is. The iPhone 4 is quite capable of taking adequate images in relatively dim light, and you may prefer the look of these to images captured with the flash.

▶ **On** Is your subject lit from behind, with the real subject essentially in shadow? You may want to try using a *fill flash* technique as a way to fill the shadow areas of the image with light. Tap **On** to ensure the flash fires, even if you're in the noonday sun in Panama.

Front-Facing Camera (iPhone 4)

The iPhone 4 actually has two cameras—one on the back of the phone (like all iPhones) and one on the front (just for the iPhone 4). Too good to be true? Pretty much. The front-facing camera is perfect for using with the iPhone 4's FaceTime video calling, but you don't really want to use it for still photography; it captures images at 640 × 480 pixels, which is far below what you'll get from the 5-megapixel camera on the back of the iPhone. The front-facing camera makes it a lot easier to snap self-portraits, but that's about all. If you must give it a try, just tap the camera icon with two arrows at the top of the display.

Viewing Photos on Your iPhone

As you're taking photos, you'll often want to inspect them in detail (or delete the ones you hate). You'll also want to show off your images to friends, family, and maybe even clients. The iPhone's 3.5-inch screen (which is measured diagonally, like a TV) displays images at 960 × 640 pixel resolution (for the iPhone 4) and 480 × 320 pixel resolution (for other models). Either way, they look awesome (though the images are not displayed at full resolution).

To look at the photos you've taken with your iPhone, here's what you do:

1. Tap the **Photos** app.
2. Choose **Camera Roll**, which is where the iPhone keeps photos taken with the camera (as shown in Figure 1-12). If you've already synced your iPhone to your computer, you may also see albums of images transferred from your computer.
3. By flicking a finger up or down the screen, you can view the photos you've taken with your iPhone camera.
4. Tap the photo you want to view.
5. Flick the screen left or right to view other photos you've taken.
6. Tap the screen to view the photo controls. You can delete an image by tapping the trash can icon.

FIGURE 1-12: *The Camera Roll displays the images you've taken with your iPhone camera.*

You can also view a photo right after you take it by tapping the thumbnail of the image at the bottom of the Camera screen.

Up Close and Very Personal

The iPhone lets you zoom in on photos to inspect the details. Here's how:

1. Double-tap the portion of the photo you want to zoom.
2. Drag your finger around the screen, without lifting it, in order to pan around the image.
3. Double-tap again to return the image to its normal size.

You can also zoom in on a photo with the iPhone's wow-inducing pinch-and-spread technique:

1. Hold your thumb and forefinger together, touch them to the iPhone screen, and then spread them apart, and you'll zoom in on the image, as shown in Figure 1-13.
2. To zoom out, reverse the gesture, bringing your fingers together.

Photo Albums

When you tap the Photos app, you'll see all the photo albums on your iPhone, as shown in Figure 1-14:

▶ **Camera Roll** These are the photos you've taken with your iPhone.

▶ **Photo Library** This contains all the images copied from your computer when you synced your iPhone (discussed later in this chapter under "Using iTunes to Sync Photos to Your iPhone" on page 19).

▶ **Albums Synced from Your Computer** When you use iTunes to sync photos from your computer to your iPhone, you can choose to transfer specific albums of images. These albums are listed below the Camera Roll and Photo Library on your iPhone, as shown in Figure 1-14.

To view the images in a photo album, follow these steps:

1. Tap the name of the album.
2. Scroll through the album until you see an image you want to view.
3. Tap the image.
4. Use your finger or thumb to flick from one image to another.
5. To view a horizontal image full-screen, just rotate your iPhone 90 degrees into landscape mode.

FIGURE 1-13: *With the pinch-and-spread technique, you can zoom in on the details of a photo.*

FIGURE 1-14: *The Photos app displays your albums.*

The Camera Roll

The Camera Roll isn't like your other albums in the Photos app. It's not just a bunch of images transferred from your computer (and stored safely elsewhere); these are the images you've snapped with your iPhone camera—your iPhone photography—and includes images you have manipulated with various iPhone apps. Delete an image from the Camera Roll, and you risk saying goodbye to it—forever.

Controls for Emailing and Sharing a Single Photo

As you're scanning through your photos, you may decide to do something with that stunning (or not-so-stunning) image of yours—namely, email it or share it. The iPhone gives you easy access to those controls. After you open an image, just tap the ⬆ button, and then select one of these options, as shown in Figure 1-15:

FIGURE 1-15: From any image, tap ⬆ to see several sharing options.

▶ **Email Photo**   This will open the iPhone's Mail program and drop your photo into an email message. You can add whatever text you like.

▶ **MMS**   This drops the image into a Multimedia Messaging Service (MMS) message.

▶ **Send to MobileMe**   If you have an account with Apple's MobileMe service, you can upload the image there.

▶ **Assign to Contact**   Take photos of your friends and colleagues, and then you'll see them pop up on the iPhone screen when they call you.

▶ **Use as Wallpaper**   You can use an iPhone photo as your phone's background image.

When emailing images, the iPhone gives you a set of choices for whether to email a full-resolution photo or a downsized one. After all, if you're just sending a friend a throwaway image from last night's party, you may not want to waste the bandwidth on a 2MB photo file. Here are the choices (as shown in Figure 1-16), with approximate dimensions (the precise size depends on the image):

▶ **Small**   320 × 240 pixels

▶ **Medium**   640 × 480 pixels

▶ **Large**   1280 × 960 pixels

▶ **Actual Size**   This is the full-resolution image.

If a friend sends you an image in an email message, you're able to save that image to your Camera Roll (or copy it for use in another app). To do this, just tap the image in the email message, and then select Save Image, as shown in Figure 1-17.

FIGURE 1-16: *Your iPhone also indicates the file size for each image size.*

FIGURE 1-17: *Saving an image sent to you in an email message*

Emailing, Deleting, and Copying Multiple Photos

When you're viewing photo albums, you're able to email, copy, and delete batches of photos. Here's how to work with multiple images, as shown in Figure 1-18:

1.   From the Camera Roll or one of your albums, tap the ⬆️ button at the top of the screen.
2.   A new series of buttons appears at the bottom of the iPhone screen. The Delete button is available only from the Camera Roll. You're not able to delete images from albums on your phone; you have to remove them from the albums on your computer (or chose not to sync those albums with your iPhone).
3.   Check the images you want to share or email, copy, or delete.
4.   Tap **Share** (to send via email or MMS), **Copy** (to include in another app), or **Delete**. You're able to email a maximum of five images in one message.

You can also delete individual images from your Camera Roll. Just select the photo, tap the Trash icon, and then confirm you want to remove it by selecting **Delete Photo**.

FIGURE 1-18: Tap the ⬀ button from one of your albums, and you will be able to check images to share, copy, or delete.

Watch a Slide Show

If you want a slide show, you can use the one built in to the Photos app. From any album, just tap an image, tap the slide show arrow, which looks like a play button (▶), and the slide show will begin. You can rotate your iPhone as the slide show is playing to switch between horizontal and vertical images.

To adjust the slide show's settings, as shown in Figure 1-19, take these steps:

1. Tap **Settings**.
2. Tap **Photos**.
3. Choose the time each slide displays, the transition, whether you want to shuffle the slides (as opposed to displaying them in album order), and whether to repeat the show after all slides are displayed.

FIGURE 1-19: You can adjust the slide show controls from the Settings app.

Places

Your iPhone camera tags your photos with the location where they were taken (unless, that is, you don't want it to) and embeds this information in them. You can then view images by location with a feature called Places. Here's how to do this with the Photos app:

1. Tap the **Photos** app, and then tap **Places** at the bottom of the screen.
2. A map appears, with red pins marking locations with photos (Figure 1-20). Tap a pin, and you'll see how many images are tagged for that location. Tap the arrow in the blue circle to view those images.
3. From the map, double-tap or use the pinch-and-spread technique to zoom on a particular area. As you zoom, additional pins will likely appear, because the location data is displayed more precisely.

FIGURE 1-20: *By tapping Places, a map is displayed with red pins for locations with photos.*

Faces and Events

If you use Apple's iPhoto or Aperture software, you will have the option of viewing your photos by tapping **Events** and **Faces**—features that sort your images by occasion and by individual. (The Faces feature uses face detection technology to find people in your photos.) For these features to work on your iPhone, you will need to synchronize Events and Faces using iTunes. The Events and Faces icons won't appear within the Photos app if you don't synchronize your Events and Faces (or if you're not using a Macintosh computer).

Transferring Your iPhone Photos to Your Computer

After taking a bunch of photographs with your iPhone, you'll probably want to transfer them to your computer for any number of reasons:

► **Safekeeping**   After all, you're less likely to lose your computer than your phone.

► **Backing up**   With your photos on your computer, you can back them up to an external hard drive or online backup service.

► **Organization**   Once your photos are on your Mac or Windows computer, it's a lot easier to sort them into albums and tag them with people's names.

✳ **NOTE:** Like other digital cameras, your iPhone camera embeds information known as *EXIF (exchangeable image file format)* data in your images, which is viewable through most desktop photo editing and organization programs.

Here's the trick to getting your iPhone photos onto your computer: Think of your iPhone as a digital camera. When you connect it to your computer, your computer will say, "Hey, I have a camera connected to me" (well, the message will likely be a bit less personal), and it will ask to transfer the images from your Camera Roll.

All of this means you'll likely want to continue using whatever software you're already using to store and organize your photos. If you're not using any software (or web-based tools) to organize your photos—if you've just been dumping images in folders on your hard drive—then now is the time to get started. By using a program such as iPhoto or Photoshop Elements, you will have much easier access to them in order to print them, find them, or do any of the other tasks enabled by digital photography, such as making photo mugs or photo books.

To transfer your images to your computer:

1. Connect your iPhone to your computer with the USB cable.
2. If you own a Mac, iPhoto will likely open, and you will be able to choose to import all your Camera Roll images or only selected images. If you own a Windows computer, you will be asked what photo-editing and organization software you want to use to import your photos, depending on what you have installed on your computer.

3. After the images are transferred, you will be asked whether you want to delete the images on your iPhone or keep them, as in Figure 1-21.

FIGURE 1-21: *Once your Camera Roll images are transferred to your computer, you will be asked whether you want to keep them on your iPhone.*

✳ **NOTE:** Think you use iTunes to transfer photos to your computer? Guess again. Though you use iTunes to sync photos *to* your iPhone—that is, to transfer photos from your computer to your iPhone—iTunes plays no role in copying photos from your iPhone to your computer.

Using iTunes to Sync Photos to Your iPhone

If you own an iPhone, then you're already using iTunes to sync your phone to your computer. You have no choice, after all: The iPhone doesn't really work without iTunes. Along with the other magic iTunes performs (backing up your phone, for instance), you can use iTunes to transfer photos from your computer to your iPhone. That means you can have thousands of photos on your phone, including images taken with your SLR, snapshots from your friends, or even scanned

black-and-white photos of your grand-
mother from the old country.

By selecting your iPhone in iTunes,
you can tweak the settings for syncing
photos from the Photos tab, which is your
route to transferring images from your
computer to your phone. Once synced,
these photos will appear within the Photos app (see Figure 1-22).

To synchronize your photos to your
iPhone, follow these steps:

1. Connect your iPhone to your com-
    puter with the USB cable, and open
    iTunes.
2. Select the **Photos** tab.
3. Depending on your operating sys-
    tem and the software installed on
    your computer, you will be able to
    choose to sync images from iPhoto,
    Photoshop Elements, Photoshop
    Album, or Aperture. You can also
    choose to sync photos from folders
    on your hard drive.
4. Choose what albums or folders you want transferred to your iPhone, as
    shown in Figure 1-23.
5. To start the synchronization process, click **Apply**.

FIGURE 1-22: The Photo Library
displays all images synced from
your computer.

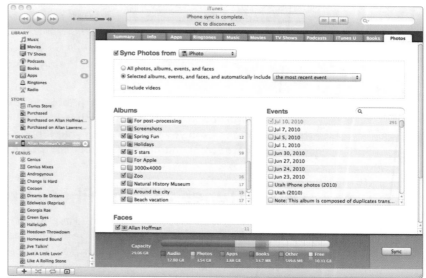

FIGURE 1-23: The Photos tab within iTunes

Accessories for Your iPhone Camera Bag

Photographers tend to be gearheads. They have lots of equipment—lenses, lights, tripods, and more. What's more, there's also the digital photography lab, which is a powerful computer outfitted with software like Aperture and Photoshop. With the iPhone, there's none of that: You have everything right on the camera. Or do you?

In fact, you may want to invest in a select number of accessories:

▸ **Tripod**   A tripod can keep your camera steady or help you take family portraits. Joby (*http://www.joby.com/*) makes a flexible, portable tripod with a special iPhone case to let you attach your iPhone to the tripod. If you already have a tripod, you may just want a tripod holder for your iPhone. G Design (*http://www.iphone-tripodholder.com/*) produces a great one.

▸ **Stylus**   An iPhone stylus is a pen-like device to let you retouch your photos (or paint) with precision. I like the Pogo Stylus from Ten One Design (*http://www.tenonedesign.com/*). But it's also very easy to make your own primitive stylus, using a damp Q-tip pinched at the tip.

▸ **Waterproof enclosure**   Aquapac (*http://www.aquapac.net/*) produces awesome waterproof cases for iPhones—a fun way to snap images in the ocean or a pool (see Figure 1-24).

▸ **Extra battery**   You don't want your battery to run out during an iPhone photography expedition. Think about buying an external battery pack, like those from Mophie (*http://www.mophie.com/*).

▶ **Skin**   Want to give your iPhone 4 the look of a real camera? Then think about buying an iPhone skin—essentially a sticker to apply to your phone. As you can see in Figure 1-25, I'm a fan of the Leica look-alike iPhone skin from PetaPixel (*http://store.petapixel.com/*).

FIGURE 1-24: *Here's a photo I took while body-surfing in the ocean.*

FIGURE 1-25: *Your iPhone 4 will truly have a camera look with an iPhone skin.*

Just don't go crazy purchasing iPhone accessories. After all, the fun of iPhone photography is how liberating it is, and there's nothing liberating in lugging around a lot of equipment.

The iPhone Photography Credo

iPhone photography is all about freedom. There are no heavy lenses, no cables or camera bag, and no crazy mess of dials and controls. Shorn of cumbersome gear, you're free to experience the world, to see it with wonder, and to capture whatever strikes you as funny or strange or beautiful. Your camera is always with you, and when the moment strikes, you go for it. There aren't a lot of rules. In fact, there aren't any rules.

But there is an evolving credo among fans of iPhone photography, and it goes something like this:

▶ Embrace the camera's constraints.

▶ Snap what you see—record your world.

▶ Do it all on your iPhone.

That means it's not really iPhone photography if you're offloading your images to your computer and laboriously applying blurs and filters with Photoshop. You take the photo with your iPhone, and you make any tweaks or adjustments, if you like, with your iPhone. (You may even publish it right from your iPhone.) It's spontaneous, and it's all about capturing your world and sharing what you see with this amazingly versatile camera.

2 Customize Your iPhone Camera

You're about to start assembling a photographic toolkit that's like something from a photographer's dreams. Just think about it. You have this bare-bones camera as part of your phone, and now you're going to transform it into something much, much more—a customizable camera with a handheld digital darkroom and a publishing system to share your images with a worldwide audience, straight from your iPhone. Without spending a whole lot of money, you'll have a camera that's far beyond anything earlier generations of photographers would have imagined.

There's just one catch: It's your job to turn it into that camera.

With the iPhone, you have the chance to build your dream camera. Other cameras have the feature set you get when you buy the camera; the iPhone camera's feature set is determined by the apps you choose. Yes, that's right—you add features to your camera by adding apps. The possibilities are endless, limited only by the creativity and industriousness of app developers around the world and by you, because you're the one to decide what your dream camera really is.

Building Your Dream Camera

Before apps—yes, there was actually a pre-app era—the iPhone camera wasn't much of a standout among smartphones. Then apps came along and changed all that. As developers created thousands of programs to give the iPhone camera the features it was missing and to make it possible to edit photos with tools rivaling those for desktop software, a new field of photography materialized from these innovations: iPhone photography (or, as it's sometimes called, *iPhoneography*).

Thousands of photography apps are now available, and companies and indie developers keep creating new ones. These apps are breathtakingly diverse in what they do, and they cater to everyone, from the 10-year-old comics junkie looking to create comic strips to professional photographers using the iPhone as a way to compile signed model releases for corporate clients. Photography is a broad category, and you'll find it helpful, as you assemble your iPhone camera bag, to have a sense of the different types of photography apps available:

- **New camera features** These apps include a self-timer, burst mode, and other discrete camera features. (Covered in this chapter.)

- **Image editors** A version of Photoshop is available for the iPhone, and it's just one of the many options for editing photos by adjusting the exposure, saturation, contrast, and other image characteristics. (Covered in Chapter 3.)

- **Single-effect apps** These are specialized apps for producing images with one effect, such as panoramas. (Covered in Chapter 4.)

- **Filters** These apps apply filters in order to add a sepia tone, turn a color image into black-and-white, and produce other post-processing tricks (see Figure 2-1). (Covered in Chapter 4.)

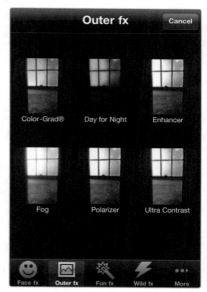

FIGURE 2-1: *The Photo fx app lets you choose a photo and then preview how it will look with various effects applied.*

- ▶ **Retro cameras** An ingenious cadre of apps can turn your iPhone camera into retro cameras of yesteryear. (Covered in Chapter 5.)

- ▶ **Fun photo apps** Use these types of apps to paint on your photos, add a thought bubble above your friend's head, and so on. (Covered in Chapter 6.)

- ▶ **Geotagging** These are apps for handling the iPhone's location data within photos. (Covered in Chapter 7.)

- ▶ **Sharing and community** Be social with your iPhone photos, via blogging and sharing. (Covered in Chapter 7 and Chapter 8.)

- ▶ **For professionals** These are tools for the pros, such as apps to calculate exposure for digital SLRs. (Covered in Chapter 9.)

- ▶ **Utilities** These include tools to help you print, transfer photos to your computer, and do other photo-related tasks. (Covered in several chapters.)

Many other apps also use the iPhone's camera, but you would never classify them as photography apps. The Amazon app, for instance, lets you snap an image of a product and then zaps back a listing of that very same product at Amazon, based only on your iPhone photo. Useful, sure, but it's not really photography.

A Crash Course on Photography Apps

Before you start building your dream camera, you need to know about apps, from how to download them (well, you probably know that already) to what semi-obscure settings lurk behind specialized photography apps.

Downloading Photography Apps

Chances are, you've already downloaded and purchased apps on your iPhone. After all, apps have come to define the iPhone experience. As you encounter the names of apps in this book, you'll often want to grab them from the App Store. Here's how to find them by searching the App Store on your iPhone:

1. Tap the **App Store** icon to enter the store.
2. Tap the magnifying glass labeled **Search**.
3. Enter the name of the app.
4. Tap the blue **Search** button.
5. Scroll up and down the list of apps for the one you want, as shown in Figure 2-2, and then tap to select it and view additional details.

FIGURE 2-2: Search for apps mentioned in the book in the App Store.

Both free and paid photography apps are available. Prices vary, but photo apps often cost $0.99 to $2.99. *Lite* versions of paid apps may be available for free in order to let you test the app (or a downgraded version of it) before you decide whether you want it. Of course, you don't want to get too riled up about the cost of apps. Many of them extend your camera's capabilities at a bargain price.

✳ WARNING: Don't be too much in a rush to abandon the Camera and Photos apps that came with your iPhone as you uncover nifty apps with whiz-bang features. The Camera and Photos apps do a first-rate job of taking full-resolution images and keeping them organized. Before you opt to use other apps instead, be sure any substitutes are doing an equally outstanding job of capturing top-notch images and preserving them.

The iPhone's photography apps can be addictive. Once you're hooked on them, you'll probably want to seek out others. Here's how to look for photography apps at the App Store on your phone:

1. Tap the **App Store** icon to enter the store.
2. Tap the **Categories** icon and label at the bottom of the screen.
3. Scroll down to Photography, and then tap the **Photography** category to open it.
4. You will then have the chance to view the top-selling paid apps and free apps, as well as view the most recently released apps (by choosing Release Date), as shown in Figure 2-3. The latter is a smart way to learn about the latest from photo app developers.

FIGURE 2-3: *Browsing the App Store's photography apps*

You can also view the photography apps from iTunes on your computer. From the iTunes Store within iTunes, choose the Photography selection from the App Store tab.

What to Consider When Buying Apps

Buying a $2.99 photography app really isn't a momentous decision. Even if you rarely use it, the purchase isn't going to break the bank, but that's not really what's at stake here. When you're buying apps—and then deciding to add them to your photographic tool set, typically to help you snap photos or edit them—you're making a decision about what sorts of photos you'll be capturing and preserving.

Consider these criteria when evaluating photography apps:

▶ **User reviews** Consult the user reviews and star ratings at the App Store. No app is universally lauded, and sometimes the user reviews are of questionable value, but by scanning them, you can get a sense of the app's quality.

▶ **Online reviews** What do the reviewers at *Macworld* and other sources have to say about the app? Those reviews are not the last word, but Googling for the app in question and the word *review* can help give you a sense of the app's quality.

▶ **Resolution** Look for details about whether the app produces full-resolution photos. See "Resolution, Resolution, Resolution" on page 28 for details.

▶ **Interface** What's the quality of interface—the buttons, icons, and other controls used to operate the app? With the iPhone, you want an easy-to-use interface that doesn't stray too far from what you have in other apps. Images of the app's screens and controls are available at the App Store (as shown in Figure 2-4), often giving clues about whether the app will be a gem or junk.

▶ **The developer** Visit the website for the app and its developer. If you have a question, email the developer. Many app developers are extremely responsive to questions and requests from users.

FIGURE 2-4: Screenshots from the IncrediBooth app indicate the quality of the app's design and functionality.

Resolution, Resolution, Resolution

I've said it before, and I'll say it again—*resolution matters*. iPhone apps don't always produce images at full resolution—the maximum resolution your iPhone camera can handle—and even if an app is capable of full-resolution images, you may have to select this as an option, sometimes in a none-too-obvious location. It's completely easy to forget to do this and then realize later—maybe much later—when you're printing your images and wondering why the results are ugly and unusable.

Follow these guidelines when buying and installing apps:

▶ Look for apps able to generate images at full resolution. App Store descriptions sometimes include this information.

▶ Avoid those that capture only low-resolution images.

▶ Check the app's settings to make sure the app is preserving images at your iPhone model's maximum resolution.

Now, you might reasonably ask, if the iPhone camera is capable of snapping full-resolution images, why would so many apps, especially newly minted ones, capture images at something far less than the camera's capabilities? Good question. Unlike the Camera app, which just captures the image, other apps often process the images in ways that tax the iPhone's software and hardware. It's considerably easier to do that with a low-res image than with a high-res one, without having the iPhone stall or crash. As anyone who's used Photoshop knows, if you're adding effects to a multimegabyte photo, you can easily sit in front of your computer and stare at the wall as Photoshop does its magic. With your phone, you probably have a lot less patience, so app makers don't want to frustrate you by tying up your iPhone.

Understanding Photography App Controls

Just because your photography apps reside on your iPhone, don't expect them to all work the same way. They don't. Just as you need to adjust when moving between other programs (and websites) on your computer—from Photoshop, say, to Flickr and then to iPhoto or Picasa—you need to do the same when switching between iPhone photo apps. Thankfully, many photo apps are streamlined tools designed to have relatively gentle learning curves. They also often have similar icons, buttons, and other controls.

Expect to encounter the following options, depending on the app:

▶ **Take a photo or edit an existing one**   With many apps, especially those for editing images and applying filters, you're given a choice of whether you want to take a new photo or use an existing one stored by the Photos app. There's no standardization among these labels, as shown in Figure 2-5. To select a photo from the Photos app, you'll typically see a button labeled Select Photo, Select Image, or Photo Library (or something similar), or you'll see an icon resembling folders (to indicate photos stored elsewhere). To snap a photo, you'll often see a little camera icon or a Take Photo button.

▶ **Save** You'll usually see an icon, such as a floppy disk or a swirly arrow, for saving the image to your Camera Roll.

▶ **Share or send** The option to share on social-networking sites or send as an email is often represented by an envelope, as shown in Figure 2-6.

FIGURE 2-5: *The PictureShow app provides clear labels whereas the Lo-Mob app uses the icons at the bottom-left to indicate the choice between taking a new image or selecting an existing one.*

FIGURE 2-6: *Tap the envelope icon in the Lo-Mob app to see various photo-sharing options.*

Settings and Options in Photography Apps

After you install an app, your first order of business is to check its settings. If you don't do it right away, you'll probably forget, and there's a fair chance that'll mean the quality of your photos will suffer (or you won't be saving them where you'd like).

You might think app settings are always located in the same spot. Guess again. As it happens, app settings are located in these two places:

▶ **The app** Fire up the app, and look for an *i* icon, a gear icon, or a button labeled Options, Preferences, Settings, or Tools (see Figure 2-7). From there, you will be able to adjust the app's options.

▶ **Settings** Your iPhone's Settings app—the one with settings for Wi-Fi, Brightness, and so forth—also stores settings for individual apps. Tap **Settings**, and then scroll down until you see your apps listed. Tap the app whose settings you want to check.

FIGURE 2-7: *Tap the i icon within the CameraBag app, and you can adjust the app's settings, such as the resolution and photo borders.*

✳ **WARNING: Some apps actually split their settings between the app itself, under a label such as Options or Tools, and the iPhone's Settings app. Just to be safe, check both after installing an app.**

The settings often include these key options (as shown in Figure 2-8):

▶ **Resolution** Apps generally give you a choice of resolutions for saving images to your Camera Roll. You may also have a choice of separate resolutions for sharing and emailing photos.

▶ **Sharing and social media** If your app connects to Twitter, Facebook, or other social media websites, you will be able to enter your username and decide whether (and when) you want to share your images.

▶ **Save original** With many apps, you snap an image, and then the app applies an effect—a night vision filter, for instance, or a 1960s look. By choosing Save Original Photo, the app will also keep a

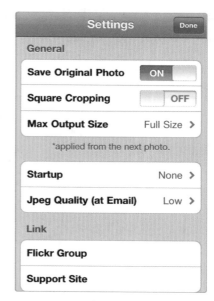

FIGURE 2-8: *The settings and options available in the CameraKit app*

copy of the image before the effect was applied. In general, choose Save Original Photo; you never know when you're going to snap an awesome shot and want an untouched copy of it available. If you don't want the image, you can always delete it from the Camera Roll.

▶ **Automatic saving**   A number of apps, especially those serving as replacements for the Camera app, do not automatically save your images when you take a photo. Instead, they present the image on your screen and essentially say, "Do you want to keep this or trash it?" If you'd rather bypass this step, then the app may offer an Auto Save option within its settings.

Organizing Your Photography Apps in Folders

Once you have a lot of apps of every imaginable type, it can be a challenge to find the one you want, when you want it. If you'd like to take or edit a photo, you don't want to have to scramble through your iPhone's *Home screens*—Apple's name for the multiple screens of apps on your phone—to find the app for it.

You have a couple of options. You can create one or more *folders* for your photography apps and then place these folders in one of your iPhone's Home screens. Or you might just choose to place all of your photography apps on one Home screen if you don't like the hassle of folders. Up to 12 apps fit on one Home screen.

I like to keep the Camera and Photos apps on my first Home screen, where they're easily accessible. I also have separate folders for different types of photography apps—utilities, replacement cameras, and so forth (see Figure 2-9). And I have one folder, *Photo Faves*, with my current favorites. I place that one in the dock at the bottom of my iPhone, where it's accessible from any Home screen. By tapping a folder, I have easy access to its contents (see Figure 2-10).

FIGURE 2-9: *Consider placing different types of photography apps in separate folders.*

FIGURE 2-10: *A folder just for camera replacement apps*

To create folders for your photography apps, follow these steps:

1. Press and hold your finger on an app you would like to include in a folder. Your apps will start jiggling.
2. Drag that app atop another one, which will create a new folder with the two apps.
3. Your iPhone automatically suggests a name for the folder—typically *Photography* for photo apps (see Figure 2-11). You can change that name by tapping the *X* in the field with the name and then typing a new name.
4. Add additional apps by dragging them into the folder. You can have as many as 12 apps in one folder.
5. Tap the **Home** button when you've finished adding apps to the folder.

FIGURE 2-11: *A new folder being created from two photography apps*

Using Apps to Add "Missing" Features to Your Camera

How do you start building your dream camera? You'll probably want to start by adding some of the features Apple left out of the iPhone camera:

▶ Self-timer

▶ Burst mode

▶ Antishake option

▶ Flash and other low-light tools

▶ Enhanced shutter button

There are two approaches to adding these features. Either you add them piecemeal, selecting narrowly tailored apps that excel in doing one thing and one thing only (for the most part), or you buy a more full-featured, multipurpose app designed to act as a replacement for the iPhone's Camera app. Either way works, but the multipurpose app option is often preferable, for a number of reasons:

▶ You'll have fewer apps cluttering your iPhone.

▶ You won't have to learn how to use a hodgepodge of apps or switch apps constantly.

▶ You'll know where to turn when you need those camera functions not built into the iPhone camera and software.

One other thing: You may save a few bucks, too.

That's not to say you should avoid those single-purpose apps. Sometimes they're truly astounding, especially in the way they reinvent something relatively simple, such as a self-timer, with umpteen options. If there's a particular camera feature you love—burst mode, for instance—then you might be thrilled to have one app devoted to just that.

Self-Timer

A stand-alone app just for a self-timer? Isn't that overkill? After all, quite a few replacement camera apps include self-timers—tools that allow you to tap the shutter button and then wait 10 seconds or so until the camera takes a shot. If you have a tripod or can prop the iPhone against another object, a self-timer lets you scoot around and get in the photo with your friends or family. Self-timers can also help you avoid blurry images caused by tapping the iPhone screen. A self-timer is a must-have feature for any camera, so it's just a question of whether you want to use a replacement camera app or a specialized self-timer app.

The iPhone's self-timer apps can be surprisingly helpful, largely because they give you so many options. Time Frame (Keren Pinkas; $0.99) lets you choose to set the timer for 3, 5, 10, or 20 seconds and whether you want it to fire off additional shots (as shown in Figure 2-12). As if that weren't enough, it lets you decide the interval between those subsequent shots, meaning you could have it take one photo after 10 seconds and then fire off another 5 shots at 3-second intervals—a great way to generate a bunch of images to ensure you capture a winner. The app even recites a countdown—an audio alert to help you arrange your hair and prepare an appropriate expression.

FIGURE 2-12: *With the Time Frame app, you're able to decide whether you want the timer to fire off after 3, 5, 10, or 20 seconds.*

Burst Mode
(Continuous Shooting Mode)

With burst mode, you're able to take a series of photos in succession, which is often useful when you're capturing a fast-moving subject (or kids who are reluctant to pose). On a traditional camera, you do this by holding your finger pressed to the shutter. On the iPhone, you need an app—either a replacement camera app or one specializing in continuous shooting. Shutter Burst (JFDP Labs; $1.99) lets you capture as many as 30 images in succession as you keep your finger pressed to the iPhone screen. It then buffers them in the iPhone's memory and lets you review the images. You can keep those you want and trash the others. The resolution of the resulting images varies (see Figure 2-13) depending on how many shots you want to take, and the app's interface isn't exactly a winner, but it can be a fun way to get just the right expression from your subject.

FIGURE 2-13: *You can snap up to 30 images in succession with Shutter Burst.*

 ## Zoom

Until Apple introduced a new version of the iPhone operating system, iOS 4, zoom was unavailable on the iPhone except as an add-on app, making zoom capabilities a much-desired camera feature. So, is there any reason to buy a zoom app if your iPhone is running the latest software? Not really, except for this: A zoom app just might include extra features you find useful. Camera Zoom 2 (KendiTech; $0.99) gives you a customizable zoom, with interesting, if not essential, controls (see Figure 2-14). One of these, a full-screen slider, lets you swipe anywhere on the screen to zoom in or out. Another setting lets you position the zoom slider at the top, bottom, left, or right of your screen. Just remember, a zoom function, even Apple's, is a digital zoom—not a bona fide zoom lens—and is pretty much the same as cropping an image, with an equivalent decline in quality.

  ## Low-Light and Flash Apps

If you own the iPhone 4, great—you have a flash. But if you don't? Then you may want to consider an app to help when shooting in dim lighting conditions. Even iPhone 4 owners may want to use these apps to snap images when the flash isn't appropriate. Just know what

FIGURE 2-14: *Camera Zoom 2's Full Screen Slider setting lets you swipe across the iPhone screen to zoom in or out.*

you're getting. Flash apps don't produce any sort of magical burst of light from the innards of your iPhone. Instead, they include filters and other features to assist you when the lighting is likely to be a problem.

Night Camera (Sudobility; $0.99) is something akin to a full-featured camera replacement, but it's geared toward helping you avoid blurry shots stemming from camera movement. The app gives you a number of ways to minimize the effects of camera movement, including a control to fire off the shutter when it detects a loud noise (see Figure 2-15). That's right: You can literally say "Cheese," and the camera will take the photo. iFlashReady (Imaging Luminary; $0.99) doesn't actually produce a flash. Instead, it processes low-light images in an effort to brighten them and draw out the highlights. It works, too. It's just not a genuine flash.

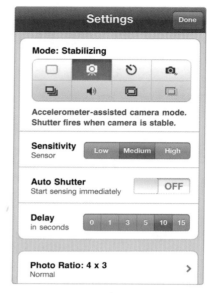

FIGURE 2-15: *Night Camera provides several modes to reduce camera movement.*

Better (and Bigger!) Shutter Button

The iPhone has a truly unconventional shutter button—just an icon on a screen, really. You can't rig the iPhone with a physical shutter button, but you can make the iPhone's shutter icon bigger; you can, in fact, turn your entire screen into a shutter button in order to avoid those times when you tap the "button" and miss your mark. With Big Camera Button (CodeGoo; free), you can tap the screen—anywhere—and the shutter fires. That's especially handy for self-portraits when you're not able to see yourself when snapping an image. (The iPhone 4 has a front-facing camera, but its image quality is far lower than the standard iPhone camera.)

A Print Button for Your Phone

With Air Photo (Sudobility; free), you can print photos right from your iPhone. You can print only one photo at a time, though a paid version of the app (Air Photo Plus; $1.99) lets you print multiple images. After you download the app, you will need to follow these steps in order to get it up and running:

1. Download and install Air Photo Server, which is desktop software for Macintosh and Windows, from the Sudobility website at *http://www.sudobility.com/*.
2. Open Air Photo Server on your computer, and then choose your print options (paper size, print quality, and other options available for your printer).
3. Tap **Air Photo** on your iPhone to open the app.
4. Tap the **Connect** button to connect to your computer. Your computer's name will appear in green letters when it's ready to go.

To print from Air Photo, ensure your computer is connected to a printer, and then follow these steps:

1. Open the Air Photo Server app on your computer.
2. Tap **Air Photo** on your iPhone to open the app.
3. Choose the image you want to print from your Camera Roll and photo albums.
4. Tap **Print** (see Figure 2-16).

If you own a printer from Canon, Epson, or HP, you may want to check out their iPhone print apps (all free): Canon Easy-PhotoPrint, Epson iPrint, and HP iPrint Photo 2.0. Unlike Air Photo, which requires the intervention of your computer, these apps let you print photos directly to printers with wireless capabilities or those connected to a Wi-Fi network.

FIGURE 2-16: *You can print photos from your iPhone with Air Photo.*

Replacement Camera Apps

Now imagine if you could have all these features in one app. Pretty nifty, right? In fact, you can have just that. Replacement camera apps bring together all the features Apple left out of the iPhone's built-in camera. Why not ditch the Camera app and use one of the apps instead? Lots of iPhone photography addicts do just that.

But not everyone. The iPhone's Camera app has some distinctive advantages:

▶ **It's simple.** You don't have to learn to use additional controls. With the Camera app, you're focused on the image.

▶ **It's fast.** All the other features of replacement camera apps sometimes slow them down, at least compared to the Camera app.

▶ **It's reliable.** It's made by Apple. You know what you're getting.

However, you may still want to use a replacement camera app, especially if it has features you crave. Several of the replacement camera apps—in particular, Camera+—go far beyond adding tools missing from the iPhone's built-in Camera app. Along with image-editing tools to apply filters and make adjustments, they sometimes provide an alternative way to save, organize, and edit images. If that's the case, the app may not save your images to the iPhone's Camera Roll automatically. Before you use one of these apps, make sure you understand whether you need to take an extra step to save images to the Camera Roll in order to transfer them to your computer or make them available to other apps for post-processing.

Avoiding Blurry Photos with an App and a Steady Hand

Remember three words: Hold it steady. You can often avoid blurry images simply by reciting those words as a mantra. You can blame the camera all you want for your blurry snapshots, but you're the one holding the camera, and there's no way to avoid blurry images if the camera is moving when the shutter fires off. What's more, the less light you have, the worse the blur will be. When you're photographing a bright scene and the shutter speed is automatically set at 1/1000th of a second, or even faster (as shown in Figure 2-17), you'll have a chance of minimizing blur. That's not the case when you're at a museum and the shutter speed is 1/15th of a second.

FIGURE 2-17: *With extremely bright light, the shutter speed may be fast enough to freeze the action in an image.*

Any solutions to this? In fact, yes—aside from the obvious one (that's holding the camera steady with two hands):

▶ **Touch and hold, then release** The iPhone camera snaps an image after you release the shutter button, not when you tap it. So either tap gently, or touch and hold the shutter button, without jabbing the camera, and then release.

▶ **Antishake shutter button** By using the iPhone's accelerometer, which senses when the phone is moving, a number of apps, including Night Camera and ProCamera, do not fire the shutter until the camera is steady. That means the camera essentially waits to take a photo until the iPhone isn't moving (or not moving much). On a boat? Trying to get your four-year-old to take your photo? Or maybe you're just realizing you have trouble holding the camera steady? You'll find this handy under any number of circumstances.

▶ **Tripod** A number of companies, such as G Design and Joby, have tripods and tripod attachments for the iPhone. In tandem with a sound-assisted shutter button, of the type available in Night Camera, you can set up your shot and then yell "Now" to have the iPhone snap the image (see Figure 2-18).

FIGURE 2-18: *The Gorillamobile tripod from Joby (PHOTO CREDIT: Joby)*

Camera+

The iPhone's tap-to-focus system is an intuitive way to adjust both the focus and the exposure of your images (see the Chapter 1). But there's a catch: You're adjusting the focus and exposure simultaneously for the same spot in the image, even if that's not really what you want. Camera+ (tap tap tap; $1.99) remedies this with an innovative interface to allow you to adjust the exposure and focus independently of each other. Here's how to operate this feature of Camera+:

1. When composing an image, touch and hold the area you want in focus with one finger. After the focus box appears, you're able to drag your finger around the screen to adjust the spot you would like in focus.
2. Without removing the finger that's holding the focus box, touch and hold the area you want exposed properly with another finger. A circle, resembling a lens opening, appears.
3. By dragging the focus box and the exposure circle around the screen—each can be dragged independently of the other—you're able to adjust the exact areas you would like in focus and exposed properly (see Figure 2-19).
4. To snap your image, remove your fingers and tap the shutter button.

Camera+ also provides other features, like stabilization and sharing options, as well as a suite of editing tools to crop images, apply filters and effects, and add borders. Like a number of other replacement camera apps, Camera+ stores images in its own camera roll, called the Lightbox. From there, you're able to edit images, save them to the iPhone's Camera Roll, copy them, or share them (Figure 2-20).

FIGURE 2-19: *Adjust focus and exposure independently with the Camera+ app.*

FIGURE 2-20: *The options available from the Camera+ Lightbox*

ProCamera

Know two things about ProCamera (daemgen.net; $1.99) for starters: It has "Pro" in its name, suggesting it's designed for serious photo enthusiasts, and it has a manual to help you use it. That doesn't mean it's a nonstarter for nonprofessionals, but it does mean you'll need to spend time learning the ins and outs in order to feel comfortable with it. Are the app's controls entirely intuitive? Not really. Yet its variety of features makes it a favorite among iPhone photography fans. Just consider the self-timer: Rather than forcing you to choose from a preset number of seconds, the app uses a slider control to let you set the time to fire the shutter from a half-second to 20 seconds after you activate it. Three options, in particular, make ProCamera a standout among replacement camera apps:

▸ **Level, compass, and grid lines** When composing a photograph, you can use ProCamera's built-in level (see Figure 2-21) to determine whether the image is aligned properly. Grid lines also help you determine where your subject should be within an image. The app includes options to alter the grid lines and replace the virtual-horizon line with a compass. You'll likely either love these features or find them an extraneous annoyance.

▶ **Image editing controls** Select Album & Studio, and you're able to edit images from your Camera Roll, including those taken in other programs. The controls allow you to adjust brightness and contrast and to apply a sepia or black-and-white effect, as shown in Figure 2-22. These controls are fairly basic compared to those available in apps devoted to image editing (see Chapter 3), yet it's useful to have them available in a camera replacement app for quick adjustments.

▶ **Independent focus and exposure controls** Like Camera+, ProCamera lets you operate the iPhone camera's focus and exposure mechanisms separately.

FIGURE 2-21: By tapping the Pro icon, you're able to adjust the grid lines and other settings.

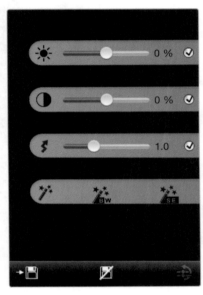

FIGURE 2-22: ProCamera's editing controls

 Camera Genius

Camera Genius (CodeGoo; $1.99) excels by keeping things simple, straightforward, and easy to understand. Among the replacement camera apps, it's a smart choice if you're looking for the essential add-ons, such as a self-timer and antishake capabilities, but you don't want the extras mucking up the simplicity of the iPhone photography experience. If that's your attitude, you'll like Camera Genius. Just tap one of the options (see Figure 2-23), and it's on or off, without having to set other variables (such as whether you want the self-timer to fire off in 5, 7, or 10 seconds).

As a plus, the app includes a succinct camera manual that defines terms such as *contrast*, *focal point*, and *perspective* and includes tips on shooting portraits and group photos. Camera Genius also lets you "stamp" your photos with the location, date, and time in a variety of formats (as shown in Figure 2-24).

FIGURE 2-23: *Selecting the timer and burst mode options*

FIGURE 2-24: *Embossing your images with the date and time with Camera Genius*

 ## Camera Plus Pro

Like ProCamera, its compatriot with "Pro" in the name, Camera Plus Pro (Global Delight; $1.99) jams lots of features into an app (and, let's face it, into the iPhone's limited screen size), aiming to serve as a replacement camera app, an editing tool, and a conduit for publishing your images to social media sites. The app also alters the typical methods for saving photos. With Camera Plus Pro (see Figure 2-25), images are saved to the app's own Quick Roll—an equivalent to the iPhone's Camera Roll. After you capture your images with Camera Plus Pro, you can open the Quick Roll to delete them or transfer them to the Camera Roll. And why, you might ask, do you need the Quick Roll? You might not, in fact, but the Quick Roll

FIGURE 2-25: *The Camera Plus Pro screen*

enables several features within the app, such as sharing to multiple social media sites (Facebook, Twitter, Flickr, and Picasa) with tags you've applied right from the app—a task that's not possible with the Camera Roll. The following are other reasons you might opt to use Camera Plus Pro (see Figure 2-26):

▶ **Point Zoom**   This feature lets you zoom into a specific area of an image by touching and holding a spot on the iPhone screen.

▶ **Media Lock**   By choosing a password, you're able to prevent others from viewing images you lock, as shown in Figure 2-27. To see or edit them, you need to enter the password.

▶ **Tags**   You can apply tags within the app as a way to categorize your photos. You're also able to search your photos by tag.

▶ **Editing**   When viewing an image from the Quick Roll, you're able to tap an Edit button to apply filters; crop or rotate; and adjust the brightness, saturation, hue, sharpness, contrast, and tint.

FIGURE 2-26: *View Camera Plus Pro's assorted options by tapping Options.*

FIGURE 2-27: *After setting a password, you're able to lock individual images in Camera Plus Pro's Quick Roll.*

Also Worth a Look

Even if you use it only occasionally, a replacement camera app is a smart addition, just as a way to add a self-timer and burst mode to your iPhone camera bag. Which one you choose is largely a matter of personal preference. Here are some other apps you might consider.

Camera One (CocoaTek; $0.99) This app places controls right on the screen you use to compose your photos—convenient, yes, but it obscures part of your image.

GorillaCam (Joby; free) From Joby, the makers of flexible tripods, here's a terrifically easy-to-use replacement camera app, as shown in Figure 2-28. The only downside? You're greeted with a very brief ad as you start up the app.

Snapture (Snapture Labs; $1.99) Along with the usual replacement app features, Snapture includes a feature, known as QuickView, to let you quickly review your recent photos.

Ultimate Camera (MacPhun; $0.99) With easy-to-understand controls, this app provides a way to automatically apply a flash effect, sepia tone, and vivid colors or to convert the image to black and white.

FIGURE 2-28: GorillaCam's streamlined controls

The Big Decision: Use the Camera App or Another App?

The App Store's replacement camera apps are designed for just that—as substitutes for the Camera app. But it turns out you can use just about any photography app as a replacement camera. That's because most photo apps give you the ability to take pictures with them, just as the Camera app does—even if the purpose of the app is to create postcards or turn your color images into black-and-whites.

So, you're wondering: Which app should I use to take pictures? There are four basic approaches to this decision, though there's a fair amount of overlap, and you'll likely find yourself experimenting with these options in order to discover what really works for you:

► **Camera app** You almost always use Apple's built-in Camera app. In this case, you would shift to another app for post-processing. Nothing matches the Camera app for its simplicity. It's for taking photos (well, video too), and that's that.

▶ **Replacement camera app**   You use one of the replacement camera apps to snap your images. In this case, you might also use the app for minor image editing, and then switch to other apps for more advanced post-processing.

▶ **A mix of third-party apps**   You use apps with specialized filters, effects, and Photoshop-like controls to snap your images, depending on what post-processing you've got planned. You know you're going to want to tweak the colors with Photoshop Express? Then take the image with that app.

▶ **Your favorite app**   If you're a big fan of a particular app, even if it's some-what specialized in its effects or filters, you might decide to use that as your default camera. So if you're gaga about TiltShift Generator, an app for pro-ducing lovely blurs, you might decide to stick with it for much of your iPhone photography. In this case, just be sure the app is able to save your original images—the image as it is before any post-processing. Many apps offer that as an option, but it's not always "on" by default.

In reality, you don't really need to choose one of these approaches. If you're like most people, you'll experiment with options, settle on a routine, and then alter it along the way. After all, just as the iPhone camera evolves, with app developers coming up with new photographic tools and improving upon existing ones, so will the way you use the camera and its photography apps.

3 Photoshop in Your Pocket

You can have Photoshop in your pocket. Literally.

It will be Adobe Photoshop Express, the version of the venerable image editor available as an iPhone app, and it will have only a fraction of the features of the desktop version, but it's still something to behold—an Adobe tool capable of adjusting the exposure, saturation, and tint, and otherwise manipulating your photos right in the palm of your hand.

What's more, several other first-rate image editors are available for the iPhone that make up for the deficiencies and missing features in the Photoshop app. No app comes close to equaling the desktop version of Photoshop, yet that's not necessarily something to lament. There's a certain freedom in escaping from all those menus and palettes you never learned how to use. With these apps, you have a digital darkroom, and you have it in your pocket. Seconds after snapping an image, it's in your hand, ready to transform in whatever way you'd like.

Your iPhone Is Your Darkroom

Consider this another step in the evolution of the digital darkroom—the transition from processing images with an enlarger and chemicals to adjusting them with a desktop computer and monitor and then back to editing them right in your hand. In fact, it's a return to something missing since the darkroom era, which is a physical connection to your photographs. Back in the day, the photographer's hands played an integral, and even intimate, role in bringing images to life; your hands touched and manipulated the negatives and the photographic paper, the enlarger lenses, and the sundry darkroom solutions. Photoshop and other tools, for all of their staggering capabilities, eliminated that physical connection to the photograph. Yet with the iPhone, you touch your photographs to adjust them, your fingers gliding over the iPhone's glassy surface as you add a blur here or adjust the tint there. It's a welcome change, and once you try it, you may not want to go back to editing images on a traditional computer.

Enhancing—and Fixing—Your Photos with Image Editors

The multipurpose image editors available for the iPhone are essential, must-have tools for your camera bag. Like desktop image editors, they have a variety of controls to allow you to alter and improve your images—though they spare you from the steep learning curve of a program like Photoshop (see Figure 3-1). What's more, these apps provide you with the experience of editing images on your iPhone, from anywhere, with the lovely wonders of the iPhone's touch screen. The iPhone, it turns out, is an outstanding tool for image editing.

* **NOTE: You can typically "stack" adjustments with image-editing apps—something that's not always possible with other iPhone apps with filters and effects. This means you can apply a sepia filter, then a border, and reduce the saturation—in whatever order you please.**

Here are some of the situations when you'll want to turn to these apps:

▶ **You need control.**   These apps give you a lot of control in editing your image, providing sliders and other mechanisms for adjusting tint, saturation, sharpness, and other factors.

▶ **You want to subtly improve an image, rather than entirely transform it.** One-effect apps have a way of taking over the process and, in a sense, imposing their own look on your images. Is that what you want? Not

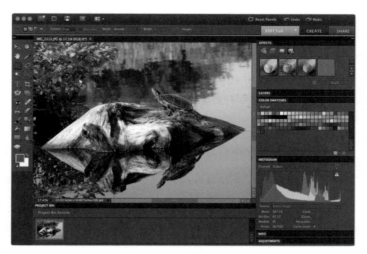

FIGURE 3-1: *Desktop image editors, even those for photo enthusiasts such as Photoshop Elements, can takes weeks or months to master.*

always. Sometimes you're really looking to make a minor, though essential, adjustment, such as cropping an image or softening the harsh lighting.

▶ **You want to prepare your photo for tweaking in other apps.** Image editors can be useful for making adjustments to images before you hand them off to another app to apply filters or other effects. If you're putting together a comic strip with an iPhone app, for instance, you may want to use an image editor to adjust the photos in advance.

▶ **You're looking to experiment.** Because image editors let you perform a variety of adjustments—and have "undo" features—these apps are ideal for trying different effects and looks with your images.

▶ **You have time.** If you're a Photoshop geek who loves to play with your images and you have the time, then these apps are yet another plaything for you.

No matter how skilled a photographer you are, you will often want to make these common photo-editing adjustments to your images:

▶ **Color** Fix the colors with Photoshop-like tools, such as Levels and Curves, as well as automatic white balance, tint, and temperature adjustments.

▶ **Contrast** Improve dull images by adjusting the contrast—the range of difference in tones from dark to light in an image.

▶ **Cropping** Alter your photo's composition by trimming it.

▶ **Exposure** Tweak too-light and too-dark photos.

▶ **Filters and effects** Use preset controls to transform the look of your photos.

- ▶ **Retouching**   Remove unwanted elements, such as a stray person, red-eye, or errant hair.
- ▶ **Saturation**   Tweak the intensity of the colors in your image.
- ▶ **Sharpening**   Increase the sharpness of your images.
- ▶ **Straightening**   Alter an image by straightening or skewing it.

So, what iPhone image editor should you choose to make these types of adjustments? This chapter covers five multipurpose image editors, each with a loyal following among iPhone photographers. Which editor you choose will largely depend on the task at hand and your own preferences. In general, PhotoForge, Photogene, and Iris Photo Suite are favored for advanced image-editing tasks, such as precise cropping, fine-tuned color adjustments, and the somewhat complex controls known as Levels. Among these "advanced" editors, Photogene is the easiest to learn and master. Perfect Photo and Photoshop Express have gentle learning curves, have fewer features and options, and are suitable for tasks requiring less control.

Now, you may be wondering, does this mean I need to buy all of these image editors? Not at all—though you won't break the bank if you do. Plenty of iPhone photographers have three or four of these multipurpose image editors on their iPhones. They may like the cropping tool in one, the black-and-white filters in another, and the exposure controls in another. By having them all available, you're able to choose just the right app for a particular image-editing task.

In the following tutorials, you'll learn how to perform the full range of tasks possible with these multipurpose image editors. Rather than covering every feature of every app, the tutorials demonstrate particular adjustments—cropping, say, or sharpening—with one app as a way to give you a sense of the essential concepts behind the task, as well as that app's interface and controls. The concepts are the same from app to app, and once you know how to make a particular type of adjustment or use a tool in one app, you'll be able to do it in all of them.

✳ *NOTE:* **If you have a favorite app that replaces the actual iPhone camera, such as Camera+ or ProCamera (see Chapter 2), that app may have adequate image-editing tools for everyday adjustments.**

Adobe Photoshop Express

The iPhone screen can handle only so many icons or options, and Adobe Photoshop Express (Adobe; free) does an admirable job of balancing the need to provide useful functionality without overloading you with too many choices, as shown in Figure 3-2. Among the iPhone's image editors, Photoshop Express is in many ways the least feature-rich of the batch—just the opposite of what you might expect, given the mind-boggling capabilities of the desktop version of Photoshop. And yet, despite its somewhat stripped-down feature set, Photoshop Express is a worthwhile addition to your iPhone camera bag, largely because of an appealing interface, intuitive controls, and a just-enough sense of the image-editing needs for many iPhone tasks.

The app is linked to Adobe's Photoshop.com service, an online hub with a web-based image editor and Photoshop tutorials. A Photoshop.com account is necessary only if you want to use the app upload and store images at Photoshop .com, as shown in Figure 3-3; you can use all of the app's editing features and save your images to the iPhone's Camera Roll without an account.

Save

Redo

Undo

Close

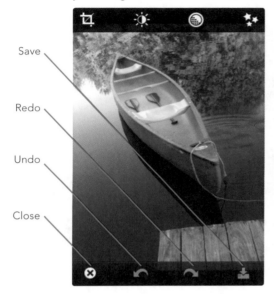

FIGURE 3-2: *Tap any of Photoshop Express's icons to reveal the available menus.*

FIGURE 3-3: *Tap Online to display any images stored at Photoshop.com.*

Saving Mediocre Photos from Oblivion

You take a lot of photos—some good, some just okay, and a lot of lousy ones. But don't just delete those lousy photos, with the lopsided composition and the out-of-whack lighting; some of them, with a bit of massaging, can turn into something more.

Cropping

You can dramatically change a photo's composition by cropping—an established, time-tested way to remove distracting elements or place more emphasis on a particular element of a photo. Whatever your ultimate goal, you're aiming to improve upon the image you have—sometimes by completely overhauling the image composition, other times by trimming an obtrusive element along one edge of the frame.

Here's how to crop an image with the Photoshop app:

1. Open the Photoshop Express app, and then tap the **Edit** button at the bottom of the screen. Tap **Select Photo** to choose an image from your albums. The image loads into the app, ready for editing.
2. Tap the **Crop** icon, and choose **Crop** from the pop-up menu (as shown in Figure 3-4). A rectangle appears, with brackets at the corners. Adjust the brackets until the image is cropped as you like, and then tap **OK** (see Figure 3-5). You're also able to press and hold your finger inside the crop box to move the cropped area around the screen.
3. Select the **Save** icon, and tap **Save and Exit** to store the image in your Camera Roll.

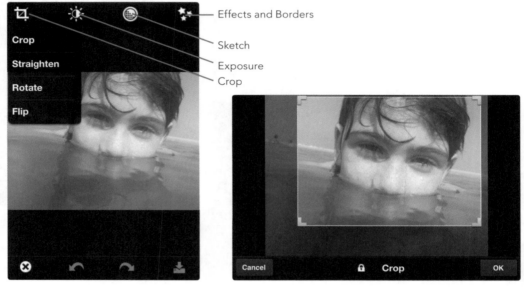

FIGURE 3-4: *Tap the Crop icon to open selections for altering your image.*

FIGURE 3-5: *Adjusting the crop in an image*

✳ *NOTE:* **When using iPhone image-editing apps, you're often able to turn the iPhone into landscape mode to make changes to horizontal images.**

Straightening (or Skewing)

The iPhone isn't always the easiest camera to hold, and sometimes you'll end up with a shot that's just slightly (or more than slightly) off-kilter. To remedy those situations, use the Straighten tool. With a quick adjustment, your image will be repaired and ready for emailing, printing, or sharing.

The Straighten tool is also useful when you want to add extra oomph to a photo by skewing it. Here's how:

1. While in the Photoshop Express app, tap **Edit** and then **Select Photo** to choose an image from your albums.
2. After you have selected the image, tap the **Crop** icon and select **Straighten** from the pop-up menu.
3. A rectangular grid appears. By dragging your finger slowly across the screen, you can adjust the angle of the image within the frame, as shown in Figure 3-6.
4. Tap **OK** when you have the desired result, and save your image.

Contrast, Exposure, and Saturation

You can often make a dull image pop by adjusting the contrast, exposure, and saturation. To make these changes with the Photoshop app, you slide your finger to the left or right across the image—an intuitive use of the iPhone's touch interface to let you make image adjustments.

1. In Photoshop Express, tap **Select Photo** to choose an image. In this case, my image is underexposed, with odd artifacts from the sunlight (see Figure 3-6).
2. Next tap the **Exposure** icon, and then select **Exposure**. Adjust the exposure by sliding your finger across the screen from right to left. You will see a number value corresponding to your action. Select **OK** to complete this action.
3. Also from the **Exposure** icon, select **Contrast** or **Saturation**, if desired, to make further adjustments, as shown in Figure 3-7.

FIGURE 3-6: *Photoshop Express includes tools to let you straighten—or skew—an image.*

FIGURE 3-7: *In Photoshop Express, slide your finger across the screen to adjust the contrast, exposure, and saturation.*

Adding Borders and Frames

After you have made other adjustments in Photoshop Express, consider adding a border or frame:

1. Select the **Effects and Borders** icon and then **Borders**.
2. Drag your finger along the border choices to view them, and then tap to select the one you want. In Figure 3-8, the **Film Emulsion** border is selected. Tap **OK**.
3. Select the **Save** icon, and then tap **Save and Exit** to store the image in your Camera Roll.

And there you have it—a dull, underexposed image rescued from the trash (as shown in Figure 3-9).

FIGURE 3-8: *Applying the Film Emulsion border*

FIGURE 3-9: *Before and after views of an image edited with Photoshop Express*

Other Image-Editing Options with Photoshop Express

Photoshop Express includes other tools to try, as well. Though the app is limited in its functionality in comparison to a desktop image editor, it's quite capable in what it does. Also consider trying these tools in the app:

► **Black and White**   Choose the **Exposure** icon and then **Black & White** for a super-simple way to produce a black-and-white photo.

► **Tint**   Choose the **Exposure** icon and then **Tint**. By sliding your finger across the screen, you're able to select a tint for the image. Your selection is displayed at the top of the screen, as shown in Figure 3-10.

► **Effects**   Choose **Effects and Borders** and then **Effects**. The options include Vibrant, Pop, Warm Vintage, Rainbow, and White Glow.

FIGURE 3-10: Giving an image a fuchsia tint

Photogene

Are you eager to do some advanced image editing with your iPhone but don't want to feel like you're sitting at your desk with Photoshop, mystified by the bounty of icons and sliders and whatnot? In that case, Photogene (Omer Shoor; $1.99) is a smart choice for the way it combines sophisticated options for manipulating your images with a straightforward interface. When you open an image with Photogene, nine icons line the left side of the screen in a neat, sensible row (see Figure 3-11). Tap any of them, and you will discover powerful tools for everything from adding thought bubbles

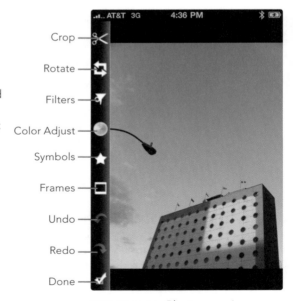

FIGURE 3-11: Photogene's image-editing controls

to images to adjusting your photos with advanced color adjustments. Like desktop photo editors, Photogene is versatile—and powerful—in what it can do. Photogene is particularly useful when you want to add a custom frame to an image.

Using Levels to Correct Image Woes

Behind every digital image is a trove of data, with endless possibilities for representing that image's one-of-a-kind rendition of color and light. Image-editing apps let you work with that data, whether by intuitive controls, such as a crop tool, or other, not-so-intuitive, ones. *Levels* falls into the latter category, but don't let that scare you away. Using Levels is just one way to view an image's data—and play with it, too.

Photogene (as well as PhotoForge and Iris Photo Suite) provides a handy, and handheld, introduction to Levels. Using Levels isn't required for image editing on the iPhone, but if you want to consider yourself among the brethren of photographers who know the ins and outs of advanced image editing, then Levels is a must.

Levels controls vary slightly from one app (or desktop program) to another, but they all share one element—a mountain-like diagram called a *histogram*. When you load an image in Photogene and then tap the **Color Adjust** tool, you'll see a histogram, which displays the distribution of colors in your photo—from black on the left to white on the right (as shown in Figure 3-12). By moving the sliding controls on the left (for black), right (for white), and center (for midtones), you're able to improve your image's appearance. Your original image is preserved in your Camera Roll, which makes it easy to get the hang of Levels by experimenting.

The Levels controls come in handy as a way to adjust an improperly exposed image or to have fine control in adjusting an image's contrast. Working with Levels is something of an art (and a sometimes complicated one, too), but you can usually improve your image by removing any empty areas on the left and right of the histogram (and allowing your own eye to guide you). Here's how:

1. Load an image, preferably one with some exposure woes, and tap Photogene's **Color Adjust** tool.
2. Look for those "empty" areas next to the slider bars (as shown in Figure 3-12), and then drag the left and right sliders toward the center, until they're located where the histogram lines begin (or thereabouts), as shown in Figure 3-13. Don't overdo it, though, or do this mindlessly, because you want to preserve your photo's atmosphere.
3. Drag the center triangle both ways to experiment with midtone adjustments until you like what you see.
4. Tap the check mark, and then select **Save**.

* **NOTE:** When you see a histogram with a big mountain in one spot, your image likely has problems and will benefit from adjustments with Levels. If the mountain is on the left of the histogram, your image is underexposed; if it's on the right, it's overexposed.

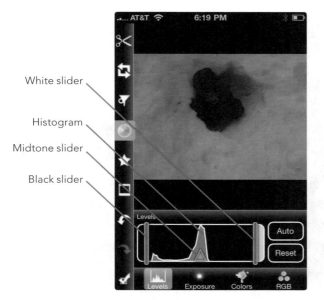

White slider

Histogram

Midtone slider

Black slider

FIGURE 3-12: *The histogram and Levels controls in Photogene*

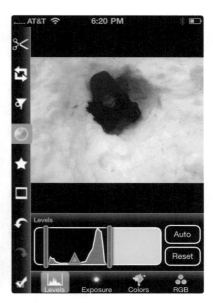

FIGURE 3-13: *Using Levels, we can now see our subject's face, and the snow is a much more natural shade of white.*

Adding a Custom Frame

Photogene includes a number of appealing frames for your images and even lets you create custom frames. Here's how:

1. Load an image into the app, and then choose the **Frames** tool, which will display the options for ready-made frames.
2. Tap **Custom** to start working on your frame, and then tap **Shape**.
3. Choose from the available shapes. Depending on the shape, you will be able to use the slider to decide its width and radius, as shown in Figure 3-14.
4. Tap **Color** to set the color for the frame (see Figure 3-15).

FIGURE 3-14: *You can decide on the width of your frame.*

5. If you like, you can add a shadow. Tap **Shadow**, and then select the type of shadow and the width. You can also choose the color for the shadow.

6. Tap the check mark, select **Save**, and you have your custom frame (see Figure 3-16).

FIGURE 3-15: *Adjusting the frame color*

FIGURE 3-16: *An image with a custom frame from Photogene*

PhotoForge

Are you longing to have the power of Photoshop in your pocket? Then Photo-Forge (Ghostbird Software; $2.99) is for you. That's not because the app actually delivers in re-creating the Photoshop experience but because it has a complete, Photoshop-like suite of image-editing and manipulation tools. You can use this app to fine-tune the color balance of your photos, apply filters and effects, and even remove unwanted image elements by retouching. Along with the power comes a certain complexity, in part because PhotoForge also includes a set of tools for creating illustrations and paintings. If you don't want to muck up your iPhone photography experience with an icon-filled image-editing app, then PhotoForge isn't for you. Yet if you're willing to explore the app—and learn how to operate its varied selection of options—then it will give you a maximum of creative control for manipulating your images.

Understanding PhotoForge's Controls and Options

Explaining this app's controls could fill a book, which is something you can't say about many iPhone apps. When you launch the app, you will notice the two sets of icons—one at the top of the screen and one at the bottom (as shown in Figure 3-17). These can be confusing, but guess what? You don't need to learn how to use all of them. Just as many photographers know how to use just a fraction of Photoshop's tools, you can try to master just a portion of those available with PhotoForge.

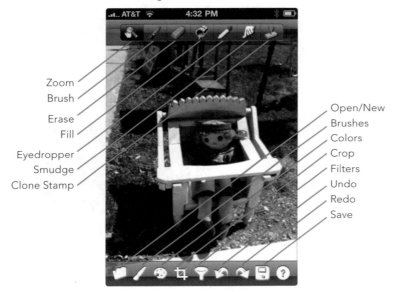

Zoom
Brush
Erase
Fill
Eyedropper
Smudge
Clone Stamp

Open/New
Brushes
Colors
Crop
Filters
Undo
Redo
Save

FIGURE 3-17: *You don't need to learn all of PhotoForge's controls and options in order to edit images effectively.*

Here are some guidelines to help:

► In general, the tools at the top of the screen, like the Eraser and Smudge tools, are used for retouching images or creating paintings; only one tool can be selected at a time.

► The menus available at the bottom of the screen provide access to key actions, such as undo and redo; they also let you refine the color and size of the Brush tool and connect you with the app's tools for cropping images and applying filters.

Changing the Aspect Ratio

Image editors typically let you adjust the image's proportions, known in photography as the *aspect ratio*—the ratio of the image's width to its height. Photos taken with the iPhone have a 3:2 aspect ratio. An aspect ratio of 4:3 is also common for still cameras. A 16:9 ratio results in a wider (or more elongated) image. And if you want square proportions for your image, choose a 1:1 aspect ratio.

Iris Photo Suite, Perfect Photo, PhotoForge, and Photogene (as shown in Figure 3-18) let you adjust the aspect ratio from their crop tools. If you're a fan of the Camera+ app (see Chapter 2), that app's editing tools provide a particularly quick way to adjust aspect ratios; the app also lets you set aspect ratios to conform to common print sizes, such as 5 by 7 and 8 by 10.

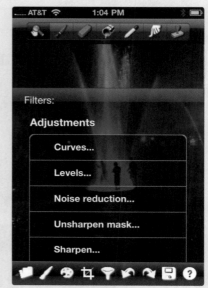

FIGURE 3-18: *The aspect ratio controls in PhotoGene*

Editing Images with PhotoForge Filters and Effects

You could almost miss PhotoForge's Filters icon when casually checking out the app's features, yet this icon—and the menu choices available from it—provide the key to altering images with PhotoForge. Ignore PhotoForge's other features and focus just on its Filters icon, and you'll have powerful tools for editing your iPhone images.

Tap the **Filters** icon to bring up the submenus, which are divided into Adjustments (editing the color, reducing noise, sharpening, and so forth) and Effects (sepia, posterize, watercolor, and others), as shown in Figure 3-19. Though many of the ready-made effects don't provide anything wondrous, especially compared to those available with specialized apps (see Chapter 4 and Chapter 5), the sophisticated adjustments available in PhotoForge give you a lot of flexibility and control in image editing. By stacking these adjustments one after another, you're able to make countless changes to your images.

Adjustments:	Effects:
Curves...	Dreamy
Levels...	Vignette
Noise reduction...	Lomo
Unsharpen mask...	Sin city
Sharpen...	Posterize
Blur	Watercolor
Simulated HDR	Oil painting
Hue/Saturation	Sepia
Brightness/Contrast	Black and white
Exposure	Night vision
Vibrance	Heat map
Tilt shift	Pencil
Auto white balance	Neon
Auto exposure	Emboss
Auto enhance	Negative
	Sunset
	BlueSky
	Television

FIGURE 3-19: *The Filters icon is the path to many of PhotoForge's image-editing options.*

Using Levels for Photo Fixes

In PhotoForge, Levels work much the way they do in Photogene, though Photo-Forge adds additional controls, similar to what's available in more advanced image-editing programs, such as Photoshop (see Figure 3-20):

► **Color Spaces** The app lets you choose your *color space*—a system for defining and displaying colors. Use the default selection, RGB (red, green, and blue), which is a common (and straightforward) option for image editing.

► **Color Channels** You can edit the levels for all colors or choose to edit each color within a color space separately. For RGB, you can edit the red, green, and blue separately.

► **Output Levels** By dragging the black and white triangles, you reduce the tonal range—and contrast—of an image.

To use Levels, follow these steps:

1. Load an image into PhotoForge, and then select the **Filters** icon.
2. Select **Levels**. You will see the histogram for the entire color space, as shown in Figure 3-20.
3. Select the different colors to see the histogram for each individual color. In this instance, the blue channel seems problematic, with the mountain of data all in one spot (see Figure 3-21).

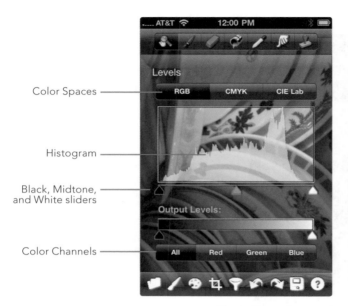

Color Spaces

Histogram

Black, Midtone, and White sliders

Color Channels

FIGURE 3-20: PhotoForge's Levels controls

FIGURE 3-21: The histogram for the blue channel in an image

4. By adjusting the white slider to the left, the unnatural yellow cast to the plates in the image is removed (see Figure 3-22).

5. Tap the **Filters** icon to complete these revisions, and then tap **Save**.

Using Curves for Control in Correcting Images

Like Levels, Curves give you a graphical representation of your image data. The name doesn't refer to any curvy lines in your photos; instead, it refers to the way you adjust a straight line into a curve to edit your image. And if Levels is algebra, then Curves is calculus. It also gives you more control than Levels in fixing your images by making it possible to adjust the tonal ranges with greater precision. Lucky for you, you won't destroy your photos with Curves. Your iPhone provides a scaled-down way to

FIGURE 3-22: Adjusting the Levels controls for the blue channel

introduce yourself to Curves—or, if you're already a Photoshop pro, to employ your know-how with your iPhone photos.

Keep these concepts in mind when working with Curves:

▶ You add points along the straight line to make adjustments and turn it into a curve.

▶ You drag a point up to increase the brightness of a tone. Drag a point down to decrease the brightness.

▶ The steeper the curve, the greater the contrast. The flatter the curve, the less contrast.

As with PhotoForge's Levels controls, you're able to choose your color space; RGB makes sense for most adjustments. Using Curves can be particularly helpful when you want to fine-tune an image by adjusting the contrast within a color channel (or even the entire color space). Here's how you can do this:

1. Open your image, and then tap **Filters** and then **Curves** (as shown in Figure 3-23). Notice the nine squares. In general, when using the RGB color space, the bottom-left represents shadows, the center represents the mid-tones, and the top-right square represents highlights.

2. Here you want to add contrast to the blue color channel, so you tap **Blue**.

3. To add contrast, you add one point in the bottom-left square and then drag down slightly. Then you add a point in the center square and drag up slightly. You also add a point in the top square and drag up a bit, as shown in Figure 3-24. The result is a curve with a very slight S shape and an image with greater contrast.

Color Spaces

Tap along the line to add points. Drag points to create a curve.

Color Channels

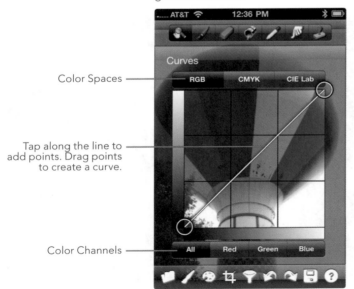

FIGURE 3-23: Using Curves to edit an image with PhotoForge

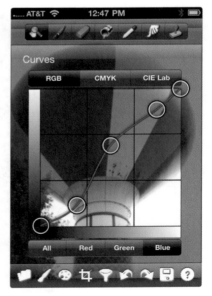

FIGURE 3-24: Adding points to create a curve and add contrast

4. Tap the **Filters** icon to complete these revisions, and then tap **Save**.

✳ *NOTE:* **With Curves, a slight change in the curve can make a big difference in your image. Don't overdo it, unless you really want to transform your image's tones and contrast.**

That's just a taste of Curves; you can use the tool in countless ways to edit images, whether you're looking for a subtle change or a more substantial one.

Retouching an Image with the Clone Stamp and Smudge Tools

You have an image with an unwanted detail—a finger straying in front of the lens, say, or a stranger distracting from the real subject of the photograph. It's just not always possible to crop them out. PhotoForge's Clone Stamp and Smudge tools come in handy in these situations, when you want to go beyond color and exposure adjustments and do some serious retouching.

1. Load your image with PhotoForge, and then tap the **Clone Stamp** tool. A target circle will appear. Drag the target circle atop the area of the image you want cloned, as shown in Figure 3-25.
2. Tap the **Zoom** tool. (Don't be alarmed when the target circle disappears.) Use the pinch-and-spread technique to zoom into the area of the image you want to edit.
3. Tap the **Clone** tool again, and your target circle should reappear (see Figure 3-26). Then tap the **Brushes** selection menu (along the bottom of the PhotoForge screen) to change the size of the brush (see Figure 3-27). You

FIGURE 3-25: *The Clone Stamp's target circle*

FIGURE 3-26: *Zoom into the area you want to edit.*

will often want a smaller brush size for photo editing. Tap the image after selecting your brush.

4. Using your finger or an iPhone stylus, such as the Pogo Stylus, paint over the area you want to substitute with the Clone Stamp pixels. By dragging the Clone Stamp target circle to another location in your image, you're able to choose new pixels to paint, as shown in Figure 3-28.

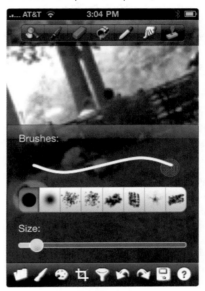

FIGURE 3-27: *Use the slider to change the size of the brush for painting with the Clone Stamp tool.*

FIGURE 3-28: *Drag the Clone Stamp tool to another image area to choose new pixels to paint.*

5. The Clone Stamp isn't perfect, and the Smudge tool can fudge your editing by creating a blur; just don't overblur an area of your image, or it will be noticeable, especially when enlarged. Select the Smudge tool, and then use your finger or a stylus to blur the edge of the area where you have used the Clone Stamp.

6. Tap **Zoom**, and adjust the zoom until your image fits the screen.

7. Tap **Save** to complete your editing (see Figure 3-29).

FIGURE 3-29: *The final image, with a frame added with the PictureShow app*

* *NOTE:* The Photo fx app, known for its filters (and covered in Chapter 4), also includes useful tools for retouching photos.

 # Iris Photo Suite

Among the iPhone's advanced image editors, Iris Photo Suite (Pranav Kapoor; $1.99) is notable for its ability to allow you to blend images with the Layers feature. That's not to say Layers is the app's only stand-out feature, because Iris includes a full complement of tools for altering your images, but its Levels controls rival those in PhotoForge. And among iPhone image editors, it has some of the most sophisticated one-touch filters, especially when you want to generate a sketch-like portrait. Iris Photo Suite can require a fair amount of exploring and experimenting in order to adjust to its interface, which isn't always intuitive.

Using ColorSense to Highlight a Color

One notable option, called ColorSense, makes it relatively simple to achieve dramatic results by preserving just one color and converting the rest of the photo to black-and-white. Iris Photo Suite makes this deceptively simple, yet it also provides controls to allow you to fine-tune the effect.

Here's how it works:

1. Open the app, tap **Edit**, and then choose your image.
2. Tap **Fx** (see Figure 3-30), and then tap **ColorSense**.
3. By dragging your finger along the color slider, as shown in Figure 3-31, you're able to determine what color will be retained.

Options: Open, Save, Layers, and Textures

Rotate, Flip, and Resize

Crop

Effects, Filters, and ColorSense

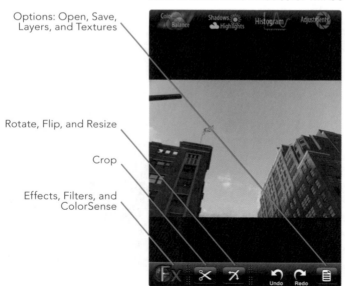

FIGURE 3-30: *The key controls in Iris Photo Suite*

FIGURE 3-31: *Choosing the shade to preserve*

4. Use the Deviation Threshold slider to adjust how selective (or forgiving) the app will be in differentiating between shades of the same color. If you want to preserve an extremely precise shade, move the slider toward 0. In Figure 3-31, a more forgiving adjustment is needed, because the sky is actually a number of different shades of blue.

5. Tap **Apply** to apply the effect.

6. Tap the **Options** button to save the image.

Using Layers to Blend Images

You can use the Layers capabilities in Iris Photo Suite to blend multiple images and create a one-of-a-kind photo construction. Here's how:

1. Tap **Edit**, and then choose your image (see Figure 3-32).

2. Tap **Options**, and then tap **Layers**. Choose **Set Layer as Base**, as shown in Figure 3-33, to set that image as your base layer.

FIGURE 3-32: The image selected as the base layer

FIGURE 3-33: To blend images, first select a base layer.

3. Tap **Options** again, and then tap **Open**. Choose an image from your albums to blend with your base image.

4. Tap **Options**, and then tap **Layers**. Choose **Blend with Base**, resulting in an image that's placed over your base image (see Figure 3-34).

5. You're now able to choose how to blend the images. Tap **Blend Mode**, and then select among the options, which include Darken, Soft Light, Hard Light, and other choices; you're able to experiment with these to decide what works best. Here we chose **Vivid Light** (see Figure 3-35).

FIGURE 3-34: *Another image is placed atop the base layer.*

FIGURE 3-35: *Vivid Light is chosen as the blend mode.*

6. Adjust the opacity of the blended images, as shown in Figure 3-36, until you achieve the desired result. You will typically want to reduce the opacity by moving the slider to the left, but the results vary among the different blend modes. Tap **Done**.

7. Tap **Options**, and then tap **Save** (see Figure 3-37).

PerfectPhoto

Compared to Iris Photo Suite and PhotoForge's plethora of tools and mini-icons, PerfectPhoto takes a simpler approach, with a pared-down interface that avoids overwhelming you with too many icons and options. Though not as powerful as the iPhone's more advanced image editors, it's more than sufficient for typical image-editing tasks, such as cropping and applying contrast and exposure adjustments. If you like your apps streamlined and simple, this image editor fits the bill.

Tools and Effects

To edit images with Perfect Photo, you open the app, load a photo, and then tap the **Tools/Effects** icon (see Figure 3-38). From there, you're able to toggle between tools and effects (as shown in Figure 3-39):

▶ **Tools** are PerfectPhoto's image-editing controls for cropping, exposure, color, and other adjustments.

▶ **Effects** are filters to transform your image with a particular look.

Layer:
Opacity
74
Blend Mode:
Vivid Light
Done
Layer
Base
Cancel

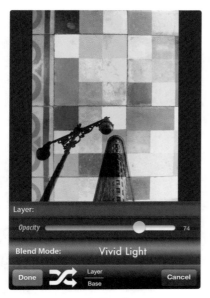

FIGURE 3-36: *Adjusting the opacity*

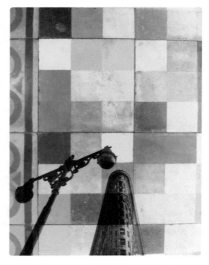

FIGURE 3-37: *The final, blended image*

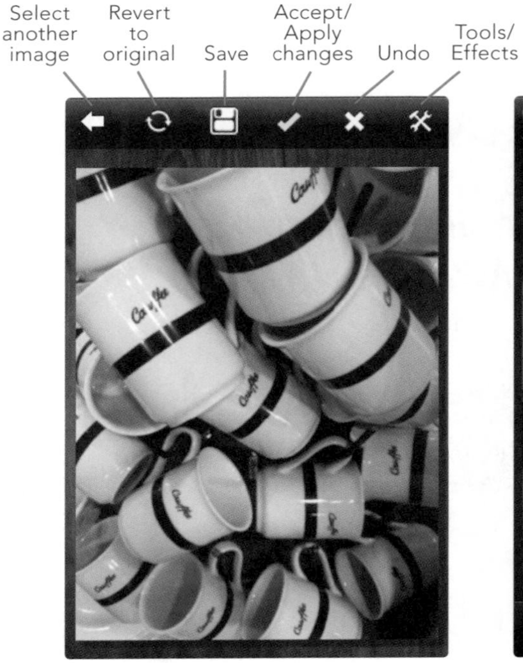

Select another image
Revert to original
Save
Accept/ Apply changes
Undo
Tools/ Effects

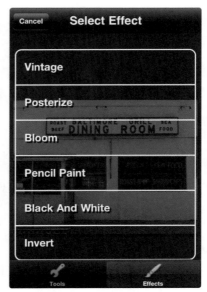

FIGURE 3-38: *PerfectPhoto's Tools/Effects icon and other controls*

Cancel
Select Effect
Vintage
Posterize
Bloom
Pencil Paint
Black And White
Invert
Tools
Effects
Tools:
Preview
Rotate/Flip
Crop
Alignment
Brightness/ Contrast
Gamma
Exposure
Shadows
Highlights
Levels
Hue/Saturation/ Lightness
Color Balance
Color Temperature
Sharpen
De-noise

FIGURE 3-39: *You're able to toggle between tools and effects in PerfectPhoto. The tools are listed to the left, and the effects are shown on the right.*

Sharpening an Image

Sharpening an image won't fix your truly blurry images, but it can help bring areas of an image into sharper focus. Here's how:

1. Load your image, tap the **Tools/Effects** icon, and then scroll down and tap **Sharpen**.
2. Sharpen the image by dragging the slider to the right toward + (see Figure 3-40).
3. Tap the **Apply Changes** check mark.

* **WARNING:** Sharpness filters don't always produce the desired results, especially if you overdo it. The results may appear just fine on your iPhone, yet when you see the image on your computer screen or on a print, you realize you made the photo worse, not better. Don't go wild with the sharpen filters available in image-editing tools, because you may regret it.

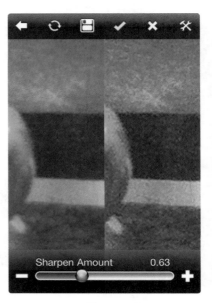

FIGURE 3-40: *Sharpening an image by dragging the slider to the right*

Automatic Adjustments—and Improvements—with a Few Taps

You may want to improve an image, but you don't have the inclination, or maybe the time, to use a Photoshop-like image-editing app. In those cases, consider using an app designed to rescue your photos automatically, without any manual adjustments required; you just open your photo, and it's rescued from oblivion. These apps' automated fixes are particularly useful for images with exposure and color problems. The apps also typically include tools to allow you to refine the results.

PerfectlyClear

Here's one of those whiz-bang apps to trot out when you want to impress your friends. After loading a photo into PerfectlyClear (Athentech Imaging; $2.99), the app automatically presents a modified version and lets you compare the improved image with the original by sliding your finger back and forth across the screen (see Figure 3-41). Tap to the left of the screen, and you'll see the Before version; tap to

Transferring Full Resolution Photos to Your iPhone

When you transfer an image to your computer and then delete it from the iPhone (as you may do in order to avoid overloading your Camera Roll), you may be losing the chance to edit it effectively with the iPhone. That's because images transferred back to the iPhone's Photos app, via iTunes, aren't necessarily transferred at their full resolution, as discussed in Chapter 1. As a workaround, you can use Photo Transfer App (ERCLab; $2.99) to transfer full-resolution images from your computer into your Camera Roll, where you can edit them with your iPhone photography apps. Photo Transfer App is also a helpful utility for transferring photos between an iPhone, an iPod touch, and an iPad with the use of a Wi-Fi connection.

the right, and you see the After version. By tapping the bar at the far right of the screen, you'll bring up an options panel to make manual adjustments, as shown in Figure 3-42, though you'll often achieve amazing results just by sticking with the automatic adjustments generated by the app.

FIGURE 3-41: *By sliding your finger from one side of the screen to the other, you can view the adjustments to your photo with PerfectlyClear.*

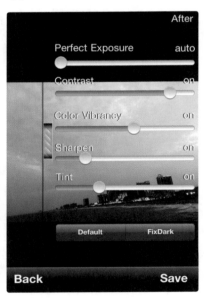

FIGURE 3-42: *PerfectlyClear lets you tweak the app's automated adjustments.*

Auto Adjust

As its name suggests, Auto Adjust (Joe Macirowski; $0.99) also provides automatic improvements to your images by adjusting their color and exposure. You open an image from your Camera Roll or Photo Library, and Auto Adjust presents you with a new version for you to save or tweak (see Figure 3-43). The app is particularly adept at correcting problems with underexposed or washed-out images.

You've Only Just Begun

You can certainly use these image-editing apps on their own, because they have powerful tools for tweaking—or transforming—your images. Load an image into PhotoForge or Photogene, and you can go wild with the filters, effects, and other options. But don't think you need to use these tools as both

FIGURE 3-43: *Auto Adjust makes automatic adjustments to your image's color and contrast and then lets you edit those values. (PHOTO CREDIT: Dianne Rosky)*

the starting gate and the finish line for your image editing. These tools are infinitely flexible, and sometimes you will want to employ them for a minor correction to the color, for instance, before you make additional adjustments. Once an image is saved to your Camera Roll, you can do anything you want with it, including load it into another app—and another, and another—in order to make further adjustments. Because that's so easy with the iPhone, you will often want to use these image-editing apps in tandem with other photography apps, such as those discussed in Chapters 4, 5, and 6. Image editors are adept at prepping an image (by cropping it, straightening it, adjusting the color and exposure, and so forth) before you subject it to tools designed to transform the photo with powerful effects and filters.

4

Filters, Effects, and Recipes

iPhone photography is often about instant grat-ification. You snap a photo, and a split second later, you're staring at the image in the palm of your hand. That's a thrill, but it's nothing next to the rush you'll get from grabbing that photo on your iPhone and then tapping here, swip-ing there, and transforming your image with the sort of deliciously blurred background that professionals get with their expensive single-lens reflex (SLR) cameras and lenses. You can achieve that sort of look, and many comparable ones, with just your iPhone camera and a well-stocked camera bag of iPhone photography apps. Instant gratification, indeed.

If there's a prototypical iPhone photography app, it's an app designed to do one thing and do it very, very well. That's a fair description of many of the apps discussed in this chapter. These apps don't aim to be Swiss Army knives;

they tackle one task, such as applying filters or generating panoramas, and that's it. For many iPhoneography fans, these apps (along with the retro camera apps discussed in Chapter 5) are really the heart of iPhone photography—the much-loved tools used to transform your photos.

You'll want to turn to these apps in these situations:

▶ **You want a big change.**   With many of these apps, you can transform a run-of-the-mill image into one with its own look and feel.

▶ **You're after a particular look.**   If you're a fan of a particular photographic technique, whether it's a blurred background or a panorama, there's likely an app for that.

▶ **You're looking for speed.**   Many of these apps, especially those with pre-fab filters, produce their effects quickly.

Though there's a fair amount of overlap among these apps, they can be divided into these rough categories:

▶ **Filters**   Filters are ready-made effects for your photos. When using filter apps, you don't have to fool with separate adjustments for color, saturation, and other image characteristics to achieve a particular look. That's the job of the filter, and it's already been done for you. Apply a filter, and your image is suddenly transformed to look like it was snapped in a fog or with an X-ray machine.

▶ **Advanced effects and techniques**   These apps are designed to re-create effects and techniques from professional photographic tools and processes, as well as desktop imaging programs, such as blurred backgrounds, double exposures, and panoramas.

Powerful Filters and Effects with Photo fx

Believe it or not, even in the Photoshop era, you can still buy glass filters to attach to camera lenses as a way to produce tints and special effects. Tiffen, a popular maker of traditional photographic filters, now also offers digital filter software; the company's iPhone app, Photo fx (Tiffen Company; $2.99), includes an astonishing 76 filters with 878 presets. And though the app is largely about filters, it also includes advanced image-editing tools to rival those in the iPhone's image editors (see Chapter 3). You could spend hours applying filters to your photos with this filter cornucopia and still feel like you were only getting started with it.

Using Photo fx Filters

The app makes it quite easy to apply filters when you want a speedy result and a prefab look. The hard part is choosing what effect you want for your image. Follow these steps to choose and apply a filter:

1. Open the app, and then tap the folder icon to load a photo from your Camera Roll or Photo Library.
2. After the photo is loaded in the app, flick among the choices at the bottom

of your iPhone screen to view the categories of effects, as shown in Figure 4-1. These categories include the following:

- **Film Lab** Adds grain, a bleached look, and other effects from traditional film processes.

- **Diffusion** Adds blurs, glows, and related effects.

- **Grads/Tints** Adds color tints and gradations.

- **Image** Includes a powerful mix of image-editing controls, such as auto-adjust, sharpening, temperature, and filters for sky, haze, and black-and-white effects; also included are levels controls and paintbrushes.

- **Lens fx** Simulates depth-of-field, wide-angle, close-up, and vignette effects.

- **Light fx** Adds ambient light, halo, soft light, and other lighting filters.

- **Photographic** Adjusts the tones of your photos by compensating for color imbalances in your images.

- **Special FX** Gives your photo a sepia tone, gives it an infrared look, or converts it to a pencil sketch.

3. In our example, the Film Lab category is selected (see Figure 4-1). That category is divided into subcategories. Tap one of those subcategories to view the individual filters (see Figure 4-2).

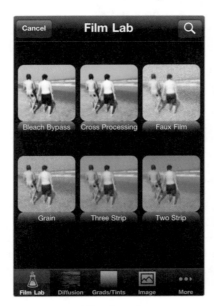

FIGURE 4-1: *Viewing the categories of effects in Photo fx*

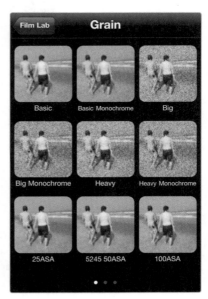

FIGURE 4-2: *Within Photo fx's filter categories, multiple options are available.*

4. After reviewing the filter options, tap a filter to select it and view a preview of how your image will look. In this case, we navigated from Film Lab to Grains and then to the 100ASA filter—a filter to approximate the effects of graininess from traditional film (see Figure 4-3). Many filters have parameters you're able to adjust. These vary, depending on the particular filter, but they may include Amount (for the filter strength), Brightness, Blur, and Temperature. You're able to adjust these parameters with slider controls.

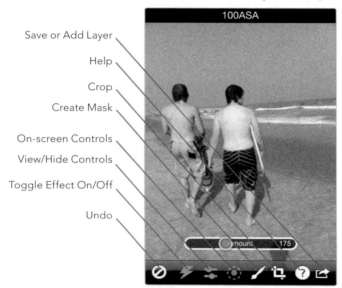

Save or Add Layer

Help

Crop

Create Mask

On-screen Controls

View/Hide Controls

Toggle Effect On/Off

Undo

FIGURE 4-3: *The 100ASA filter in action, along with key Photo fx controls*

5. To crop an image, tap the **Crop** icon. You can choose an aspect ratio by tapping the **Aspect Ratio** icon, as shown in Figure 4-4. After you adjust the aspect ratio, tap the **Crop** icon to adjust the exact area you want to crop.

6. To save the image with the effect, tap 📷, and choose **Save**.

Depending on the filter you choose, you may also be able to adjust your image with the On-Screen Control icon (see Figure 4-3), which is highlighted only for certain filters. When the On-Screen Control icon is activated, you're able to adjust the size and location of an effect, as with Light Ray 1 (see Figure 4-5).

Adding Layers

Photo fx lets you stack filters and other image adjustments one after another, which is a powerful way to achieve complex effects by using just one app. To do this, follow these steps:

1. After you have already made changes using one filter, tap 📷, and then tap **Add Layer**. You will now be able to apply additional filters. If you've already put a lot of work into adjustments with earlier Photo fx tools and want to be extra safe, you can also tap **Save** to save your image and then proceed to tap 📷 and **Add Layer**; that method will preserve the earlier version of your image with changes by saving it to your Camera Roll, just in case you botch things along the way with your new adjustments.

2. Once you have added a layer, you will return to Photo fx's filter selection screens. You can now apply additional effects and filters. Here we

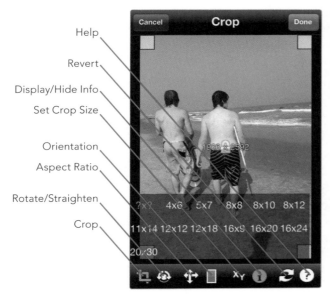

Help
Revert
Display/Hide Info
Set Crop Size
Orientation
Aspect Ratio
Rotate/Straighten
Crop

FIGURE 4-4: *Cropping an image with Photo fx*

FIGURE 4-5: *Using the On-Screen Control tool to adjust the light ray effect*

proceeded to **Film Lab**, then **Cross Processing**, and then **Slide to Print 3** (see Figure 4-6).

3. Tap **Save** to save the image, or proceed to add additional layers.

Masking Images for Complex Effects

Now imagine you want to apply an effect to just a portion of an image. That's possible with the flexible masking tools in Photo fx. In Photo fx, you apply a mask with the Add Effect or Erase Effect tools as a way to tell the app, "Apply the filter to this area and this area only." In tandem with the layers available with Photo fx, you're now able to edit images in powerful ways; you might, for instance, darken the sky—and only the sky—in an image, using the app's masking tools, and then

FIGURE 4-6: *The unusual colors generated by the Slide to Print 3 effect*

add another layer to brighten the scene in the foreground using another mask (and an entirely different filter).

Remember these key points when using masks to apply filters and edit images with Photo fx:

▶ When you opt to create a mask, you tap the Create Mask icon (see Figure 4-7), and the filter is applied to the entire image by default.

▶ Use the Erase Effect tool to paint over image areas and remove the filter from those areas (see Figure 4-8). If you want the filter to apply to much of the image, use the eraser tool.

▶ Use the Add Effect tool (see Figure 4-8) to add the filter to areas of the image. That's especially helpful when you have overdone things with the Erase Effect tool.

▶ You can also fill an outlined area with an effect (or remove the effect from an area) with the Fill icon (see Figure 4-8), used in tandem with the Erase Effect and Add Effect tools. To select an area, outline the area with the Erase Effect or Add Effect tool; use the Add Effect tool if you want the filter to appear within the area, and use the Erase Effect tool if you want to remove the filter from the area. Next tap the Fill icon, and then tap inside the outlined area.

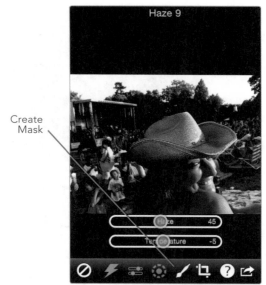

FIGURE 4-7: *The Haze 9 filter applied to the image*

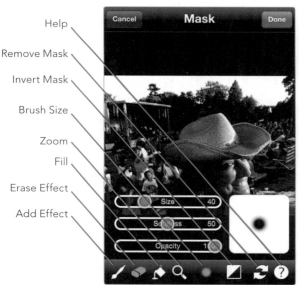

FIGURE 4-8: *The brush controls are displayed, along with the mask controls.*

To see this in action and experiment with masking, choose an image with clearly defined areas to apply (or remove) the effect of a filter. Here's how:

1. Load your image into Photo fx, and then navigate through the filters to a strong effect. In this example, we chose the Image filter collection, and then Haze ▸ Haze 9 (see Figure 4-7). The filter is applied, and you're able to make adjustments with the filter's controls—though you can also make adjustments after the mask is applied.

2. Tap the **Create Mask** icon. The effect is applied to the entire image area by default.

3. Tap the **Brush Size** icon to adjust the size, softness, and opacity of the brush, as shown in Figure 4-8. This will apply whether you're adding an effect or erasing it. You can always change the brush settings as you work on the image. Quite often, you will want to use a big brush for broad areas and then switch to a finer brush (with a soft edge) for detailed areas and edges.

4. Tap the **Erase Effect** icon, and drag your finger (or, preferably, an iPhone stylus) over the area where you don't want the filter to be applied (see Figure 4-9). As you'll see, the brush is represented by a green circle.

5. Consider these additional steps to help:

   ▸ Tap the **Zoom** icon to zoom into a particular area to make adjustments with greater detail. Tap the **Zoom** icon again to return to the Erase Effect tool.

   ▸ Tap the **Invert Mask** icon, to toggle between the masked and unmasked areas. This can help you visualize what areas you have covered and what areas remain for editing.

   ▸ To erase the filter effects from a large area of an image, outline it with the Erase Effect tool, as shown in Figure 4-10. Tap the **Fill** icon, and then tap inside the outlined area. The effect will be removed from that area.

FIGURE 4-9: *Use the Erase Effect tool to erase an effect from areas of your image.*

6. Once you have erased areas, you may realize you eliminated the effect from some areas unintentionally. You can use the Add Effect tool to paint the effect onto areas of your image, using the same techniques used with the Erase Effect tool.

7. Tap **Done** when you have completed the work on your mask. You will return to the initial filter screen, where you can make further adjustments to that filter's parameters, such as Haze and Temperature in this example (see Figure 4-11). These will be applied only to unmasked areas.

8. Tap 🔲 and then **Save** to save your image.

FIGURE 4-10: Using the Fill tool to remove the area where the filter effect is applied

FIGURE 4-11: You can adjust a filter's parameters after a mask has been applied.

Painting, Retouching, and Special Effects with Paint Brushes

The painting tools in Photo fx let you do a lot more than add colored brush strokes to your images. The app provides eight different brushes for retouching and special effects (see Figure 4-12):

▸ **Color** Select your color and add "paint" to an image.

▸ **Clone** Grab pixels from one part of an image and paint them into another area.

▸ **Blur** Blur portions of your photo.

▶ **Black and White**   Paint over areas to turn those pixels to black and white.

▶ **Mosaic**   Create a mosaic look, with tiled squares, by painting over portions of the image.

▶ **Repair**   Paint with the color sampled at the start of a brush stroke.

▶ **Red-Eye**   Remove red-eye by tapping a spot where it appears.

▶ **Scatter**   Scatter a random blast of pixels.

With each of these tools, you're able to adjust the size, softness, and opacity of the brush by tapping the **Brush Size** icon. That's a smart first step before you start painting; these tools are all about precision editing, and you'll achieve the results you want only if you select an appropriate brush size (and adjust the brush size as you make adjustments to different image areas).

Here's how to use Photo fx's painting tools, with the Mosaic brush used as an example:

1. Load an image, and then tap **Image ▶ Paint**.
2. By default, the Color brush is selected, as shown in Figure 4-13. You can now paint on your image, as you would in an iPhone painting program such as Brushes. But the real power, for image editing, materializes when you tap the **Color Palette** icon to reveal the additional brush tools (see Figure 4-12).

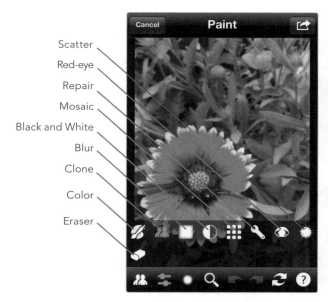

FIGURE 4-12: Photo fx's painting and retouching tools

FIGURE 4-13: Tap the Color Palette icon to view the painting tools.

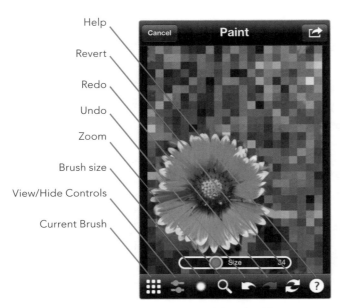

Help
Revert
Redo
Undo
Zoom
Brush size
View/Hide Controls
Current Brush

FIGURE 4-14: Use the Zoom, Undo, and Redo tools to fine-tune your work on an image.

3. Tap the **Mosaic** tool to select it.

4. Like the other painting tools, the Mosaic tool has its own special controls, which you can view or hide by tapping **View/Hide Controls**. In this example, we increase the size of the tiles produced by the mosaic effect.

5. To achieve a mosaic effect, we increase the size of the mosaic tiles and then paint over the areas where we want the effect. We can use the Zoom, Undo, and Redo tools, as shown in Figure 4-14, to correct mistakes and work in detail.

6. Tap to save the image or add another layer.

Quick and Easy Filters with FX Photo Studio

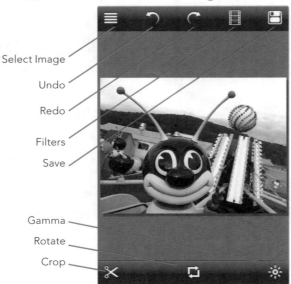

Select Image
Undo
Redo
Filters
Save
Gamma
Rotate
Crop

FIGURE 4-15: An image loaded into FX Photo Studio

FX Photo Studio (MacPhun; $0.99) includes 140 filters in an easy-to-use interface to let you apply filters quickly. The filters are varied in what they do, but overall, the app is best for those times when you want an over-the-top transformation of your photo rather than a sophisticated adjustment.

Here's how to apply a filter with FX Photo Studio:

1. Load your photo into the app (see Figure 4-15).

2. Tap the **Filters** icon, which will display the categories of filters, such as art, blur, distortion, texturize, and vintage. Tap the category you want.

3. Scroll through the filters, as shown in Figure 4-16, and then choose the one you want to view. A preview is displayed (see Figure 4-17). Tap **Apply** to apply the filter to your image.

FIGURE 4-16: Filters are divided into categories in FX Photo Studio.

FIGURE 4-17: After you choose a filter, a preview is displayed.

4. Tap **Save** to save the image to your Camera Roll (see Figure 4-18).

    Also think about trying these features of FX Photo Studio:

    ▸ Tap the **Star** icon (see Figure 4-16), and you're able to save a filter as a favorite for easy access from the app.

    ▸ You can stack filters with the app. After you apply a filter, you're able to continue applying additional ones, giving you a way to produce your own customized effects.

    ▸ Choose the Frames category of filters, and you can give your image a frame with butterflies, cupids, or flowers.

FIGURE 4-18: An image saved with FX Photo Studio

Blur, Selective Focus, and Fake Miniature Effects

Professional photographers often use big lenses—and their significant know-how—to capture an image with the subject in focus and the rest of the image blurred. If there's a photographic look suggesting the photographer's expertise (and equipment), then this is it. There's even a term for this type of blur, *bokeh*, from the Japanese word for blur. With SLRs that have interchangeable lenses and manual controls, a blur is typically achieved by narrowing the *depth of field*—the area of an image that's in focus. Techniques vary for doing this, but it's often accomplished by having a wide aperture (or lens opening) for the image; the wider the lens opening, the narrower the depth of field. (The type of lens used matters, too.) With the iPhone, the aperture is fixed, so you'll use an app, TiltShift Generator (Art & Mobile; $0.99), to give your image a wonderful blur. TiltShift Generator isn't the only app for blur effects—others include BlurFX and Focusoid—but it's a favorite among iPhoneographers. What's more, you can use TiltShift Generator to provide other special effects, such as re-creating the look of a miniature toy model.

Creating a Background Blur

To simulate the blurred background look, you essentially want to fool the viewer into thinking you used an SLR with manual camera settings and an expensive lens to focus on your subject and create a blur in the rest of the image. Choose an image with a person (or object) in the foreground to give this a whirl. Here's how:

1. To load your image, tap **New** and then **Album** (for images in your Camera Roll and Photo Library), as shown in Figure 4-19.
2. Tap **Blur** to adjust and apply the blur. You're able to choose either a radial blur (with the in-focus area defined by a circular shape) or a linear blur (with the in-focus area defined by parallel

FIGURE 4-19: *Tap Album to load an image from your iPhone photos*

lines). With a radial blur, the area in the inner circle will be in focus. The area between the inner and outer circles will have a gradual blur. (These tools function in the same way for linear blurs.) Use the pinch-and-spread technique, with two fingers, to adjust the overall area of the focus; use the slider to adjust the area between the inner and outer circles. You can also position the focused area by dragging the circle around the screen.

3. Tap **Color** for sliders to adjust the image's saturation, brightness, and contrast (see Figure 4-20).

4. Tap **Vignette** to apply a vignette around the edges of the image.

5. To save to your Camera Roll, tap **Save** (in the lower-right corner of the screen) and then **Save** again (along the left side of the screen), as shown in Figure 4-21. You achieve wonderful effects by creating background blurs with Tilt Shift Generator (see Figure 4-22).

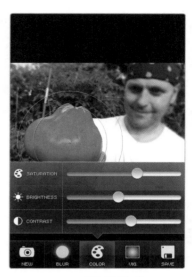

FIGURE 4-20: *TiltShift Generator offers sliders to adjust saturation, brightness, and contrast*

FIGURE 4-21: *The app's controls for saving to the Camera Roll*

FIGURE 4-22: *A background blur created with TiltShift Generator*

Fake Miniature Model Effects

Ever go to a model-train show around the holidays? Wow, the crowds! Everyone loves miniature models, with their brightly painted figures and painstaking details. Close-up photos of models, with their oversaturated, dream-like look, have their own appeal. TiltShift Generator lets you re-create the look of a close-up photograph of such a scene right on your iPhone, using everyday images. The name of the app, in fact, is a tribute to the traditional method for achieving this effect, known as *tilt-shift photography*—a method requiring tilting the lens (or sometimes the film plane) to generate the effect. Even with an app, the iPhone version of tilt-shift photography requires a bit of planning in order to have a photo that's right for the fake miniature effect. Don't expect to take any image and be able to transform it with a fake miniature look. The look often works best when you have an image shot from above, looking down upon a scene with your "miniature" elements, such as buildings and roadways. You're essentially trying to re-create the look of a model shot from slightly above.

Once you have the right photo, follow these steps:

1. Load your image, and then tap **Blur** (see Figure 4-23).
2. Select the area for your blur by choosing the linear or radial blur tools, and then adjust the area for the blur. In general, for a fake miniature look, you want to have the scene in the foreground in focus, with other image elements farther away blurred, as shown in Figure 4-24.

FIGURE 4-23: *Objects in the foreground help you achieve a fake miniature look.*

FIGURE 4-24: *Applying a blur*

3. Next, add saturation and contrast. Because models are typically lit by artificial light and painted with bright colors, additional saturation and contrast heighten the miniature model look.
4. Apply a vignette, if you like.
5. Save your image to the Camera Roll (see Figure 4-25).

Selective Focus

The typical image with a background blur includes a person (or object) in the foreground with the background blurred. But that's far from the only use of Tilt-Shift Generator. Even in images without a standard composition for a background blur, you can achieve amazing results with the app—though you may need to experiment a bit to get things just right. By choosing one spot in the image as the focal point and blurring the rest—a style known as *selective focus*—you're able to generate a photo with a lot of style and atmosphere. What you select as the focal point really depends on the image. Unusual effects can be generated by subverting the viewer's expectations of what would be in focus. Here's an image (see Figure 4-26) where a number of image elements are equidistant from the camera lens and so would be expected to be in focus, yet the blur has been positioned to focus your attention on one particular subject.

FIGURE 4-25: *A fake miniature look created with TiltShift Generator*

FIGURE 4-26: *The use of selective blur to highlight one image element*

Panoramas

The iPhone's panorama apps let you stitch together images right on the camera. They're fun, they're a breeze to use, and the results are nothing short of spectacular. As a general rule, you want to stay in one spot when creating a panorama; after taking one shot, rotate the camera, aiming for an overlap of a quarter to a third of the image between shots. Each of these three apps has its own way of generating panoramas, and the results are distinctive, too.

AutoStitch Panorama

AutoStitch Panorama (Cloudburst Research; $2.99) assembles photos from your Camera Roll or Photo Library into a panorama. Rather than having smooth edges, AutoStitch panoramas often have a quirky, one-of-a-kind look to them (see Figure 4-27). If people are moving around in the image, they may appear as ghostlike apparitions in the resulting panorama.

FIGURE 4-27: *A panorama created with AutoStitch*

Before you assemble a panorama, review the app's options by tapping **Info** and then **Options**. These adjustments are available:

▸ **Resolution**   The Standard setting will generally produce excellent results, but if you want more control, select Advanced, where you're able to choose to generate a panorama with a maximum output size of up to 20 megapixels.

▸ **Blending**   Set this to Best to reduce blur between overlapping photos. Set it to Standard for the quickest results. Set it to None to generate a less polished—and more idiosyncratic—look.

▸ **Auto-Exposure**   Set this to On to adjust for exposure changes between adjacent images.

Here are the steps to assembling your panorama after you have snapped the photos:

1. Open AutoStitch, and then navigate to photos you want to include. If you have just taken the photos, they will be in your Camera Roll.
2. Tap a photo to add it, as shown in Figure 4-28. Tap additional photos to add them, too.
3. Tap **Stitch** to create the panorama.
4. As it's being created, you're able to pan and zoom around the screen to inspect your work in progress (see Figure 4-29).
5. If you like, you can crop your image by tapping the **Cropping** icon (see Figure 4-30), and then adjusting the crop, and finally selecting the **Crop** button.
6. Tap ⬆️ to save the image or share it.

FIGURE 4-28: *Adding photos to AutoStitch to create a panorama*

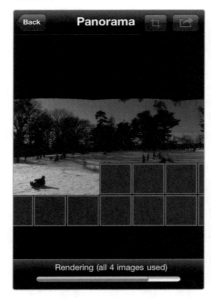

FIGURE 4-29: *A panorama being created by AutoStitch*

FIGURE 4-30: *You can crop your panorama if you want it to have sharply defined edges.*

Pano

With Pano (Debacle Software; $2.99), you create your panoramas by taking your photos right from the app. The app provides guidance along the way to help you match one photo to the next. Here's how:

1. Open the app. Pano will instruct you to take your first photo. For a panorama with a landscape view, tap the icon to toggle between landscape and portrait views, as shown in Figure 4-31.

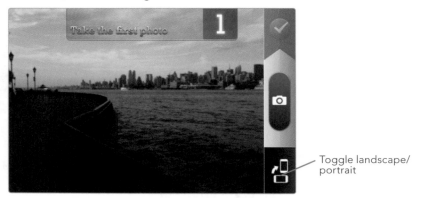

Toggle landscape/portrait

FIGURE 4-31: *You can choose to create your panorama in landscape or portrait view with Pano.*

2. Tap ⬤ to snap your first image.
3. To help you match your next photo with the one you just snapped, Pano overlays a transparent portion of the previous image on the iPhone screen. When you match up the previous image with the one you're about to snap, tap ⬤.
4. Continue taking additional images with the same method. If you mess up, you can back up by tapping a swirly arrow on the Pano screen to retake an image or start over.
5. To complete your panorama, tap the check mark. Your panorama will be saved to your Camera Roll (see Figure 4-32).

FIGURE 4-32: *A panorama created with Pano*

You Gotta See This!

You Gotta See This! (Boinx Software; $1.99) is notable for letting you capture a scene without even snapping individual images. You just scan your camera around the scene, and the app magically assembles a panorama-like photo for you. When you're at a stadium concert—or the Grand Canyon—this is the app to use, but it's also fun just to produce an unconventional representation of a particular location.

1. Open the app. With your camera in your outstretched arm, tap ⬛, and then move the camera around to scan the scene, which is visible in a preview window, as shown in Figure 4-33. Don't move the camera too fast. If you do, a yellow (and then red) border will appear around your preview window.
2. Tap ⬛ again to stop recording your scene.
3. You Gotta See This! allows you to choose among several collage-like styles for saving your image (see Figure 4-34).

FIGURE 4-33: *You Gotta See This! displays a preview of the scene as you scan it with your camera.*

FIGURE 4-34: *The app lets you choose among different styles.*

4. Tap ⬛ to save or share (Figure 4-35).

FIGURE 4-35: *A scene captured with You Gotta See This!*

 # High Dynamic Range (HDR) Imaging

HDR photography can produce eye-popping images by blending multiple photographs (see Chapter 1). Though the iPhone 4 includes built-in HDR capabilities, other iPhone models do not, and even iPhone 4 owners may prefer the HDR results from Pro HDR (eyeApps; $1.99), which blends two photos of a scene to produce an HDR image (see Figure 4-36). Because you're using two images of the same scene, you need to keep the camera steady; objects in the foreground, in particular, may appear blurred if there's any camera movement from one image to the next.

FIGURE 4-36: *The HDR image provides even lighting and detail throughout the image, dramatically changing the exposure and overall effect, especially when compared to an image not processed with an HDR tool.*

The app allows you to choose from Auto HDR or Manual HDR. With Auto HDR, you simply snap your image, hold your iPhone steady, and the app does the rest for you. With Manual HDR, you need to use your own judgment in selecting bright and dark areas of the scene. Here are the steps to taking an HDR image with manual controls:

1. Open the app, tap **Manual HDR**, and then compose your image. Tap in a bright spot within the frame, and then tap **Accept**.
2. Tap somewhere dark in the image, and then tap **Accept**.
3. Make adjustments to the brightness, contrast, saturation, and warmth, as desired, and then tap **Save**.

Color Adjustments and Effects with Mill Colour

Image editors and filter apps let you adjust the color of your images, but sometimes you're after an effect or technique that's even more specialized than what those apps offer. In those instances, consider using Mill Colour (The Mill; free)—an app that's devoted to color adjustments and effects. Built by The Mill, an Oscar-winning visual-effects company, the app is a marvel of interface design and sensitivity to the ways minor color adjustments can completely redefine a photograph. It gives you two ways to approach image editing—either through preset filters (called Looks) or by adjusting colors in a meticulous manner. Applying the Looks is simple and straightforward: You just load an image, tap **Looks** (see Figure 4-37), and then flick among the various filters.

For fine-tuning, tap **Colour Controls**, and follow these steps:

1. Tap **Mode**, and select what image characteristic you want to edit, as shown in Figure 4-38: Saturation, Gain (bright areas), Gamma (midtones), or Lift (dark areas). For each of these, a slider with numbered gradations will appear, allowing you to make adjustments as you view the effects on your image.
2. For Gain, Gamma, and Lift, make adjustments to the red, green, and blue channels separately in order to have precise control of your alterations (see Figure 4-39).
3. Tap **Done** and then **Save** to save the image to your Camera Roll.

FIGURE 4-37: *The Looks button provides access to Mill Colour's preset filters.*

FIGURE 4-38: *You're able to edit Saturation, Gain, Gamma, and Lift separately.*

FIGURE 4-39: *For precise control, edit the red, green, and blue channels individually.*

 Double Exposures

In the age of Photoshop, the genuine double exposure is a relic. Pre-Photoshop, a photographer would expose two images on the same frame of film (or photographic paper) in order to achieve a double exposure. That's no longer necessary; you can simply create a new layer in Photoshop (or another desktop image editor) to superimpose one image over another. But for a blast from the photographic past, open Night Camera (Sudobility; $0.99), select its **Settings** icon, and then choose **Double Exposure** mode (see Figure 4-40). After you take your first image, that image will appear as a transparent overlay when you snap the second image. You never really know whether the results of a double exposure will be worth anything, but that's part of the fun.

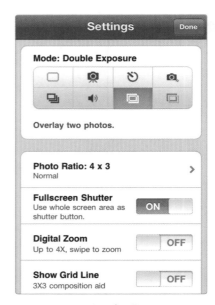

FIGURE 4-40: *Night Camera, set to Double Exposure mode*

Adding a Border or Frame to Your Photo

Frames can give your photo a truly stylish look, especially when you use an app, such as Lo-Mob or PictureShow (both discussed in Chapter 5), to re-create the retro effects from negatives, film emulsions, and borders from earlier film formats. They're a particular favorite among professional photographers enamored with iPhone photography, because they have a certain nostalgic allure. Many apps, for everything from editing images to applying off-the-wall filters, have the ability to add borders and frames, but there's a catch: You may need to apply one of the app's filters or effects along with a border or frame. But some apps let you apply frames without filters or effects, which means you can edit your image in whatever app you choose and then add the frame as a last step.

Here are some of the best apps for borders and frames:

▶ **Lo-Mob**   Tap the **i** icon, and then tap **Settings**. Under Effects (see Figure 4-41), set Process frame to **On** and the other settings under Effects to **Off**. Now, when you load an image in Lo-Mob, the app will apply a selection of frames to your image, but it will not apply the app's other effects (as shown in Figure 4-42).

FIGURE 4-41: Adjusting Lo-Mob's Settings in order to apply frames but not other effects

FIGURE 4-42: Lo-Mob's News Emulsion border replicates the look of a print from a medium-format film negative.

▶ **Photogene**   Create custom frames, as discussed in Chapter 3.

▶ **Photoshop Express**   Tap the **Effects/Borders** icon, and then tap **Borders**. Drag your finger across the options to view the available borders.

▶ **PictureShow** Swipe through the effects for your image until Original is selected. (This is 0 of the 27 effects.) Then select **Style**, and swipe horizontally to view the different frames, which include such awesome-looking effects as 120 Reversal, OldMat, OldFashioned, VintageDust, and Burned (see Figure 4-43).

FIGURE 4-43: *Images from PictureShow, with the Convex Blur and 120 Reversal frames*

Taking Things to the Next Level with App Recipes

Sometimes one app just isn't enough when editing images on the iPhone. Just as you're able to stack filters, one after another, with an app like Photo fx, you're also able to use multiple apps when editing a single image. To do this, you edit the photo in one app, save it to your Camera Roll, and then switch to another app to edit the saved version. You can run your image through as many apps as you would like, with a couple of caveats:

▶ The resolution of your image may decrease if you use apps that reduce its image size.

▶ Overall image quality may deteriorate as a result of too many effects and filters being applied.

In general, ask yourself what you're really after—playing with apps (which is, of course, a fun pastime!) or creating a wonderful photo—if you're using more than four or five apps.

You will often want to use multiple apps for these purposes (and generally in this order):

- **Cropping** You might use Photogene, Photoshop Express, or any other image editor to crop or straighten an image before running the image through an app designed to transform the photo with a filter or effect.

- **Color** Mill Colour is a favorite among iPhoneographers looking to get the colors just right before applying a frame or another effect; you can use other image editors for this purpose, too. You might also want to adjust the color after processing an image with another app as a way to fine-tune it.

- **Transformation** Use an app, like Color Process or TiltShift Generator, to really transform your image in a big way.

- **Frames** Applying a frame is typically the last step in editing an image.

Creating app recipes is far more of an art than a science. You try one thing and then another until you stumble upon a combo that works (see Figure 4-44 and Figure 4-45).

Here are seven recipes worth trying:

- **PhotoForge ▸ SwankoLab ▸ PictureShow** Use PhotoForge to adjust your image with levels or curves, and then revamp things by adding the faux chemicals in SwankoLab. Use PictureShow for a border style appropriate to the SwankoLab look.

FIGURE 4-44: *In this recipe, we started with Photogene and wrapped things up with Lo-Mob.*

- **Mill Colour ▸ TiltShift Generator ▸ Photogene** Fine-tune image colors with Mill Colour, and then apply a blur effect with TiltShift Generator. Wrap things up by adding a custom frame with Photogene.

- **Photoshop Express ▸ Lo-Mob** Sometimes an app duo is what you really need. Straighten your image, crop, and correct colors with Photoshop Express, and then add a frame with Lo-Mob.

- **Cross Process ▸ Mill Colour ▸ Photoshop Express** Use Cross Process for that otherworldly cross-processed look, and then fine-tune those colors with Mill Colour. Use Photoshop Express for the final touches, with any straightening or cropping necessary.

- ▶ **Perfectly Clear ▸ Photo fx ▸ Lo-Mob** Run your photo through Perfectly Clear for a quick improvement, and then make more substantial changes with Photo fx and Lo-Mob.

- ▶ **Perfectly Clear ▸ Plastic Bullet ▸ MonoPhix ▸ Diptic** Knowing you'll finalize things with Diptic, an app for combining images, you need to do a fair amount of planning to prep your photos before firing up Diptic. Use a mix of apps for those images, depending on the look you want, and then open Diptic to combine them into a multiframe photo.

- ▶ **Photogene ▸ Spica ▸ Photo fx ▸ Photoshop Express** Straighten an image with Photogene, and then give it a high-contrast black-and-white look with Spica. Use Photo fx to adjust the monochrome look and then Photoshop Express to add a border.

FIGURE 4-45: *This photo used PhotoForge for cropping, Cross Process for color edits, and then Photoshop Express for final adjustments.*

Once you start working with apps in this way, you will probably find you're turning to the same stable of apps for your own recipes. Some iPhoneographers just about always add a blur with TiltShift Generator. Others invariably use Mill Colour for color adjustments. You'll inevitably have your own set of go-to tools. But as the tools evolve and new and innovative apps emerge, you will likely find yourself tweaking your recipes and the way you edit your images.

5 The Retro Look

I have a bunch of junky old cameras inside my iPhone, and I love every one of them. Consider this one of the curious by-products of technological progress. Even though we love our techie gadgets and their shiny innovations, we yearn for the outdated, glitch-prone tools of yesteryear: Typewriters and their smudgy ribbons. Turntables with their clicks and pops. The vintage cameras, obsolete photographic films, and darkroom processes from a time when either you dropped your skinny cartridge of 110 film in a mailer and hoped for the best or you experimented with a do-it-yourself darkroom in a closet. The results were often mixed, with plenty of chances for botched results (messed-up processing from the dude at the Fotomat, fixer stains on your black-and-white prints). And now, strange as it may seem, we miss all of those mistakes, and we're doing everything possible to bring them back.

Through a sleight of hand made possible with hyper-creative apps (and what seems, frankly, like a miraculous mix of coding prowess and creative mojo), you're actually able to replicate the plastic cameras and darkroom foul-ups of earlier decades on your iPhone. It may seem like a weird way to take photography into the future, but you can use your iPhone, this marvel of electronic circuitry and software code, to blast into photographic history and produce botched photos, streaked with darkroom chemicals and looking like they just popped out of a shoe box your eccentric, photography-obsessed grandfather kept on a shelf for decades. You can turn your photos into Polaroids from the 1970s, Depression-era prints with wonderfully sloppy borders, or just about any look you want from photographic history. And the results? Your photos will be the most enchanting images you've ever captured from any camera you've ever owned.

Step into the iPhone's Photographic Time Machine

The iPhone camera is chameleon-like in its ability to turn itself into a seemingly infinite variety of cameras and film formats. One moment it's a Polaroid SX-70, the next it's a Lomo LC-A, and soon it's a junky yet decidedly hip instant camera conjured out of the wild dreams of a hipster dude from Brooklyn. This is all part of the historical fantasyland that's iPhone photography. By gazing back into photographic history, iPhone apps like PictureShow, Hipstamatic, and CameraBag have invented their own cameras, films, and flash types, with names like Lolo and Williamsburg, to mimic the look of old-time film stocks and vintage—and sometimes malfunctioning—cameras. The wonderful Hipstamatic camera (really, an app) is essentially a vast and ever-evolving fictional world—a nostalgic fantasy about what it was like to own a lousy plastic camera and try to make the most of the sometimes random effects you got from it. A more genuinely historical approach is taken by other apps, such as Film Lab, with its attempt to reproduce the look of photographic films of the past. You can even have a faux darkroom, with the chance to mix chemicals and see the results, courtesy of SwankoLab. Hundreds or thousands of films and chemicals have been used over the past 100 years, and the iPhone is now bringing them back, one by one, via apps designed to resurrect the tools used by photographers decades ago. Sometimes this is real, sometimes it's fantasy, and most of the time you won't really know the difference, but you'll love the results anyhow.

To 1974—and Beyond

iPhone apps take a variety of approaches to producing images with a retro look. For quick, easy-to-implement results, you'll want an app that's all about applying a filter to your images. With these apps, you load your photo (or snap a new one) and then review the ways the app is able to transform it into styles from the past.

 **CameraBag**

CameraBag (Nevercenter Ltd. Co.; $1.99) evokes a mix of cameras and films from recent decades. The app produces eye-popping results with filters such as Helga, Colorcross, Lolo, and 1974. To view your options, follow these steps:

1. Tap the **Load Photo** icon to select a photo, as shown in Figure 5-1.
2. Flick across your iPhone screen to review the filters. You can also tap the current filter name to view the other available filters (see Figure 5-2).
3. Once you find a filter you like, tap **Save** to save your photo to the Camera Roll. That's it!

CameraBag gives you several useful options, which are available by tapping the **i** icon:

▶ **Use Borders** Switch this to **Off** if you don't want borders applied.

▶ **Use Cropping** Some of CameraBag's filters automatically crop your image to replicate the look of earlier photo styles. Set this to **Off** to preserve your image proportions.

▶ **Favorite Filters** Don't like a few of CameraBag's filters? Turn them to **Off**, and you won't see them displayed when flicking from one image to the next (see Figure 5-3). These filters will still be available from the list of filters available by tapping the name of the current filter.

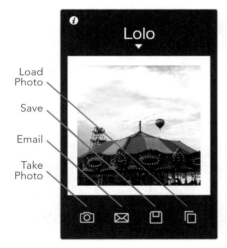

FIGURE 5-1: An image in CameraBag, with the Lolo filter

FIGURE 5-2: Tap the name of the current filter to view (and select) other filters.

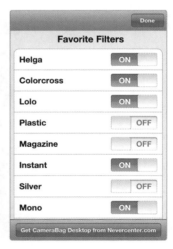

FIGURE 5-3: Select favorite filters to view when flicking through image previews.

Lo-Mob

Lo-Mob (aestesis; $1.99) takes you on a fun photographic nostalgia trip, with a strong bent in the direction of experimental techniques used by 20th-century photographers (see Figure 5-4). You can happily apply these effects without knowing anything whatsoever about the terminology (film emulsions, TtV, and so forth), or you can see this as your chance to learn something about the techniques and tools behind these wonderful effects. Here's a quick primer on Lo-Mob's categories of effects:

- ▶ **Classic Vintage**   Get square images with an assortment of retro looks.

- ▶ **35mm Film Experimentation**   Experimentation, indeed. Here's an assortment of effects achieved by placing 35mm film inside cameras meant for medium-format films, placing one film type atop another, and exploring other photographic techniques.

- ▶ **Through the Viewfinder**   Also known as TtV, the through the viewfinder technique involves capturing an image with one camera by shooting through the viewfinder of another camera, often a vintage one.

- ▶ **Emulsions**   A long time ago in a galaxy far, far way, photographers used various techniques to have prints with ragged-edged borders. Now, you can have these types of borders with your iPhone photos.

- ▶ **Instant Matic**   These effects bring back the look of Polaroids and other instant photos.

- ▶ **Contact Mask Photocards**   Get the look of old-fashioned photo postcards.

FIGURE 5-4: Images with Lo-Mob's 6x6 TTV Virage (left) and Vintage Instant (Black) filters (right)

Now, how do you get these effects? Like this:

1. Load a photo, or snap a new one.
2. Lo-Mob displays the available filters, with thumbnail previews and helpful labels describing the effects and their historical provenance, if any (as shown in Figure 5-5), such as "Contact Print of a Negative Glass Master from the 30s" (for the 30s Contact filter).
3. Tap a thumbnail to view the effect with your image.
4. Tap the image to enter Lo-Mob's Edit Mode and display mini-icons for the filter, blur, vignetting, and frame, as shown in Figure 5-6. (Not all images have all four as options.) You're able to toggle these options on or off by tapping each one—a terrific way to experiment with your image to get just the right mix of effects; an option is set On when its icon is green.
5. To adjust the framing of an image, touch and hold the screen to move the image, or use the pinch-and-spread technique to zoom.

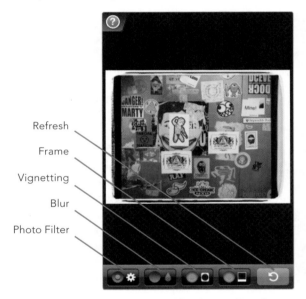

FIGURE 5-5: The app displays thumbnail previews and descriptions of its filters.

FIGURE 5-6: The News Emulsion effect in Lo-Mob

6. Once you've completed editing, tap the Refresh button (see Figure 5-6) to apply your changes and exit Edit Mode. If you want to explore other filter options, tap the filter name at the bottom of the screen, as shown in Figure 5-7, to return to the list of descriptions and thumbnails.

7. Tap the disk icon (see Figure 5-7) to save your image.

Lo-Mob includes lots of options for sharing via social media websites. To enter your information for these sites, tap the **i** icon after opening the app, then tap **Settings**, and finally enter your login details. The app's settings also allow you set the app's effects to **Off**. If you know you don't want to use the app's blur and vignetting effects, you can turn them to **Off** to avoid having them applied to your images.

FIGURE 5-7: *Tap the name of the filter to return to the thumbnail preview images.*

 ## PictureShow

With 27 styles of effects (28, if you include Original, for your raw, unfiltered image) as well as 21 borders and frames, PictureShow (graf; $0.99) makes it possible to experiment with nearly 600 combinations of ready-made effect-and-frame combos. Beyond those ready-made effects, the app offers additional controls in the form of color, brightness, and contrast adjustments, as well as the chance to add text to your images and experiment with vignettes and light effects. All of this adds up to an app that's appropriate for those times when you want to say "Give me a quick effect" and also when you want sit down and take the time to fine-tune an image.

Here's how to apply PictureShow's filters:

1. Open the app, and then load an image.
2. Flick up and down vertically to view your image with the different filters, as shown in Figure 5-8.
3. Tap **View All Effects** to scroll through a list of effects and select one from the list, as shown in Figure 5-9.
4. To save an image to your Camera Roll or to share it, tap **Share**.

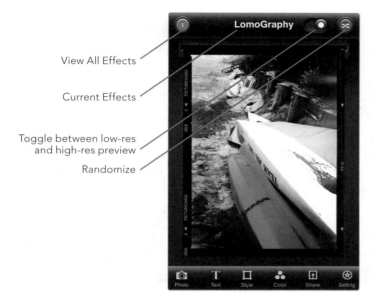

View All Effects

Current Effects

Toggle between low-res
and high-res preview

Randomize

FIGURE 5-8: *Flick vertically to view different filters and effects.*

FIGURE 5-9: *You can tap the View All Effects icon to scroll through a list of effects.*

As described in Chapter 4, Picture-Show is a terrific app for adding frames to photos. After you apply a frame, you also have a chance to add a vignette, light leaks, and noise. Here's how:

1. Load your photo, and then tap **Style**. A new series of icons will appear at the bottom of the screen, as shown in Figure 5-10.

2. To view the available frames, tap **Frame**, and then flick among Pic-tureShow's frame options. Tap one to select it.

3. After selecting a frame, tap **Vignet** to set the amount of vignetting. Adjust the slider to the left for minimum (or no) vignetting, and swipe to the right for maximum vignetting.

4. For various light effects, tap **Light**, and then flick among the light effects to view them, as shown in

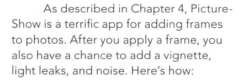

FIGURE 5-10: *You can add light effects to produce an ethereal quality in your images.*

Figure 5-10. The effects include light leaks and halation. Light leaks sometimes occur with cheap or malfunctioning cameras, when light enters the chamber where the negative is exposed. Halation refers to halo-like effects in bright areas of an image. Tap an effect to select it.

5. Tap **Noise** for additional effects approximating prints (or negatives) damaged by scratches or suffering from excessive graininess and other problems (see Figure 5-11).

6. Tap **Done** to complete your adjustments (see Figure 5-12).

7. Tap **Share** to save or share your photo.

PictureShow includes several other fun and useful ways to work with your photos:

▶ **Randomize** If you want to let the app generate random combinations of effects and frames, tap **Randomize**—a fun, quick way to get a sense of the variety of looks you can get out of PictureShow.

▶ **Add text** Tap **Text**, and you're able to add a message to your image. The app lets you adjust your font, font size, alignment, and text color.

▶ **Image editing** To enter Color Edit mode and modify your image's colors, as well as brightness and contrast, tap the **Color** button to bring up image editing controls.

FIGURE 5-11: *The noise effects in PictureShow can give your photos an aged or damaged look.*

FIGURE 5-12: *A photo processed with PictureShow and using the 135 Reversal frame, maximum vignetting, Light Leak 4, and the GrungeSoft noise effect*

Polaroids and Instant Cameras

The images from Polaroid and other instant cameras have a distinctive look. They're also something of a precursor to digital cameras in the way they provide instant gratification. With the Polaroid SX-70, for instance, you would snap an image, the print would slide out of the camera with a lovely whirring sound, and you would watch as the image materialized before your eyes. The iPhone's Polaroid-like instant camera apps don't exactly replicate that experience—they don't magically print images from your iPhone—but they do attempt to re-create the wonder of seeing an image develop as you wait and watch.

 ### ShakeItPhoto

Here's an easy-to-use app for you. You open ShakeItPhoto (Nick Campbell; $0.99), tap , and watch as the image appears before your eyes (see Figure 5-13). If you want your image to "develop" faster, you just shake your iPhone. You're also able to process photos you've already taken with the app. Just tap **Cancel**, and then tap the **Load Photos** icon—the overlapping rectangles—to select an image from your iPhone photos. It's a wonderful, no-frills experience.

FIGURE 5-13: *Photos from ShakeItPhoto (PHOTO CREDITS: Sean Kaufman)*

 ### Polarize

Polarize (Christopher Comair; free) generates images with a border resembling those produced by Polaroid's SX-70 cameras. As for the look, the app gives your images vibrant, high-contrast colors. Just open the app, tap **Load from Photo Album** or **Take a Photo**, and you've got your image. Tap the screen, and then tap **Tag** to add a label for the image (as shown in Figure 5-14). Tap the image again, and then tap **Save** (see Figure 5-15).

FIGURE 5-14: *Adding a label with Polarize*

FIGURE 5-15: *An image created with Polarize*

 ClassicINSTA

This instant app is loads of fun and versatile, too—though not quite as instant as its name might imply. With ClassicINSTA (misskiwi; $0.99), you're able to select from several "cartridges" with helpfully descriptive names, such as Vintage Sepia, Retro B/W, Damaged, and Rainbow. A certain amount of experimentation is required to uncover the results of these cartridges, and you may need to do a retake in order to get just the effect you want.

Here's how:

1. Open the app, and then tap **Camera** or **Photo Library** to snap or load an image.

2. After the image is loaded, flick among the available cartridges, as shown in Figure 5-16.

Cartridges   Print Slot   Shutter Button

FIGURE 5-16: *Choosing a cartridge with ClassicINSTA*

3. Tap the shutter button to develop your image, which slides out of the print slot.

4. Tap **Recent Prints** to view the recent images processed with the app (see Figure 5-17). If you like, you can tap **Remove** to remove prints from ClassicINSTA's Recent Prints storage area.

5. Images are automatically saved to your Camera Roll, even if removed from ClassicINSTA (see Figure 5-18).

FIGURE 5-17: *You can tap Recent Prints to view the images you've taken with the app.*

FIGURE 5-18: *An image created with the Damaged cartridge*

The Wonderful World of Hipstamatic

There are many cameras inside your iPhone but none as consistently popular with iPhone photographers as Hipstamatic (Synthetic Corp.; $1.99). Hipstamatic is a phenomenon—an iPhone camera known for the idiosyncratic, retro look of the photos generated by its selection of fake lenses and films. The app turns iPhone photography into an activity that's partly a game and partly a hipster's fantasy about the cameras of yesteryear. When you open the Hipstamatic app, you're not just taking a photo; you're making a statement about what's cool and wonderful about the world. It's something like slipping an old-fashioned camera out of your camera bag and seeing what sort of images you'll get from it.

As for the photos, Hipstamatic gives you the stunningly messy and off-the-wall look of cameras from the past—in particular, inexpensive plastic cameras. But there's not really one signature Hipstamatic look. By using various combinations of Hipstamatic's lenses (with names such as Helga Viking and Jimmy), flash types (Cadet Blue Gel, Berry Pop, and so on), and films (Alfred Infrared, Pistil, and so on), you have hundreds of combinations of effects you're able to produce.

Quick Start with Hipstamatic

Hipstamatic has a lot of options to select, but you can get started fast by following these steps:

1. Open the app, and then shake your iPhone to generate a random combination of film, lens, and flash.
2. To use the flash of your iPhone camera (or to simulate a flash effect), drag the Flash switch to the left to activate the flash. The Flash Ready light will turn green.
3. Compose your photo in the Hipstamatic viewfinder (see Figure 5-19), and then tap the shutter button.

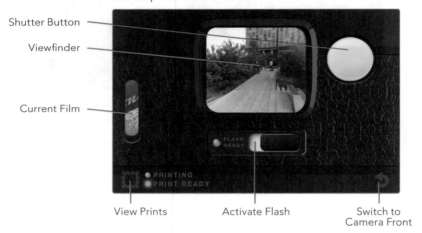

Shutter Button

Viewfinder

Current Film

View Prints   Activate Flash   Switch to
                                         Camera Front

FIGURE 5-19: *The back of the Hipstamatic camera provides access to the shutter button, viewfinder, and other controls.*

4. Wait for your print to develop. A green light will appear next to the View Prints icon when it's ready. Tap the **View Prints** icon, and you will have access to your image, as well as others from Hipstamatic (see Figure 5-20).
5. Tap your print to view the details about its lens, film, and flash, as shown in Figure 5-21.
6. To save your print (or share it), tap 📷 and then **Save to Photo Library**.

FIGURE 5-20: *Viewing your prints*

Delete

Change Camera Settings

Contests

Add to Stack

Save/Share

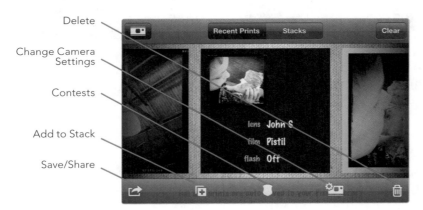

FIGURE 5-21: *Tap your print, and you can view details about the Hipstamatic settings used to capture it.*

Selecting Your Lens, Flash, and Film

You could produce a lot of fun photos by shaking your Hipstamatic camera to randomize the results, but that wouldn't actually be diving wholesale into the Hipstamatic experience. For that, you want to choose—and explore—the offbeat details of Hipstamatic's lenses, flash types, and films. In fact, a lot of the fun of Hipstamatic comes from mulling over your lens, flash, and film selections. These are wholly imaginary, but you can easily start exploring them and lose your sense of reality as the line between a real film or flash and Hipstamatic's versions starts to blur.

Just be sure to keep the following in mind (see Figure 5-22):

▶   **Lens**   The lens is where a lot of the Hipstamatic action is. It's essentially a filter applied to your image.

- ▸ **Film**   Some Hipstamatic films affect only what your frame (or image border) looks like, while others also apply a filter to your image, along with a frame.
- ▸ **Flash**   The app's flashes typically add a burst of light or color tone to an image.

FIGURE 5-22: Note the different frames to these images, resulting from the film selection. The image on the left uses the John S lens, the BlacKeys B+W film, and the Dreampop flash. The image on the right uses the Lucifer VI lens and the Pistil film, with no flash.

Here's how to select the lens, flash, and film:

1. Switch to the Hipstamatic camera front, which is where you select your lens, flash, and film (see Figure 5-23).
2. To switch your lens, swipe across your screen horizontally, and a new lens will appear.

Swipe horizontally to change lens

Switch to Camera Back

HipstaMart

Lens

Choose Flash

Choose Film

FIGURE 5-23: The front of the Hipstamatic camera includes access to controls for choosing your film, flash, and lens.

3. To view the details about a lens, tap the lens, and information about the lens will be displayed (as shown in Figure 5-24). Some lenses are included as "standard equipment" with the Hipstamatic camera; others must be purchased. The same goes for flash types and films.

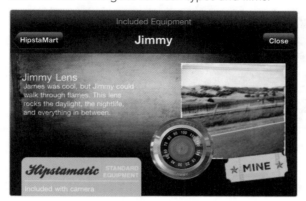

FIGURE 5-24: *Information on the currently selected lens*

4. Next tap the **Choose Film** icon. Your currently selected film will appear, as shown in Figure 5-25. As with the lens, you can tap the film to view details about it (see Figure 5-26).

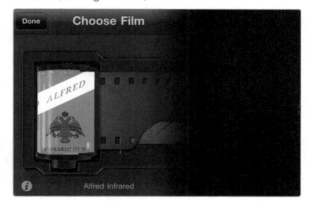

FIGURE 5-25: *The current film*

5. To switch films, flick vertically to view other film options.
6. To select a flash, tap the **Choose Flash** icon. Choosing a flash works the same way as choosing your film and lens. Review the options by flicking across the screen; tap a flash to view the details.
7. After making your selections, you're ready to take a photo. Tap the **Switch to Camera Back** icon; then compose your photo, activate the flash (if you like), and snap away.

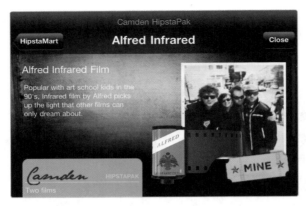

FIGURE 5-26: *Details about the current film*

Taking Things to the Next Level

You're able to take things a lot further with Hipstamatic by creating stacks of prints, buying new Hipstamatic equipment and supplies, and developing favorite lens/flash/film combos.

Stacks for Sharing—and Printing

Hipstamatic's Stacks option lets you create stacks of Hipstamatic images to share or have printed. Here's how:

1. Tap the **View Prints** icon from the camera back, and then tap **Stacks**.
2. Tap **+** to create a new stack.
3. To add photos, drag your prints onto the stack, as shown in Figure 5-27.
4. Enter a title for your stack and tap **Done**.
5. From your stack, tap , as shown in Figure 5-28, to share or send the stack via email. You can also add an image to an existing stack when viewing the print; just tap the **Add to Stack** icon (see Figure 5-21).

FIGURE 5-27: *Creating a print stack*

HipstaMart Print Shop

FIGURE 5-28: *You're able to share images or enter the HipstaMart Print Shop from your print stacks.*

6. To buy a stack of prints, tap **HipstaMart Print Shop** (see Figure 5-28), and then choose from the selections (see Figure 5-29). Prices vary, depending on the print size and the number of prints.

FIGURE 5-29: *The HipstaMart Print Shop lets you buy prints of your Hipstamatic photos and have them delivered.*

HipstaMart

Though Hipstamatic includes adequate supplies and equipment, you may want to buy new lenses, film, and flash types—essentially a way to expand your personal collection of Hipstamatic filter effects and frames. With additional Hipstamatic tools in your arsenal, you'll have even more options when snapping Hipstamatic photos.

Here's how to make purchases from the HipstaMart:

1. From the camera front, tap the **HipstaMart** icon.
2. Flick across your screen to view the items on sale (see Figure 5-30).
3. To view additional details, tap an item.
4. Tap **Buy HipstaPak** to make a purchase (see Figure 5-31).

Now your items, whatever they may be, will be available to you in Hipstamatic.

FIGURE 5-30: *Viewing items at the HipstaMart*

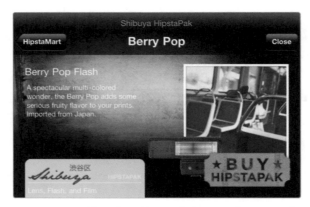

FIGURE 5-31: *Tap Buy HipstaPak to make a purchase.*

Camera Back or Camera Front?

You're able to decide whether Hipstamatic starts up with the camera front or camera back. Just tap your iPhone's Settings app, scroll down to Hipstamatic, and, under the Shooting section of Hipstamatic's settings, choose whether to activate Camera Back or Camera Front on startup. Starting up with Camera Front is useful if you're always adjusting the app's lens, film, and flash options.

Turning Off Your Flash

Got an iPhone 4? Then you may be wondering what happens when you activate the Hipstamatic flash. Does your iPhone's LED flash fire off, or not? In fact, Hipstamatic lets you decide whether to fire off your flash or not. In many cases, with Hipstamatic, you'll want one of the app's flash effects, but you won't really want your iPhone's flash to fire off. After all, Hipstamatic flash effects often add an idiosyncratic light burst to your image—even if it's an image snapped in bright daylight. To prevent the iPhone's LED flash from firing with Hipstamatic, tap the iPhone's Settings app, navigate to Hipstamatic, and turn the Disable LED Flash setting to **On**.

Creating Favorite Combos

You can have a lot of fun by experimenting with Hipstamatic and seeing what sort of effects you can achieve with different combinations of lenses, films, and flashes. But sometimes you'll stumble on one you really love, and what do you do then, other than just commit it to memory (not a bad idea, of course)? If you keep an image produced with that combo in Hipstamatic (under Recent Prints), you can apply the combo without selecting your lens, flash, and film one by one. Here's how:

1. From the camera back, tap the **View Prints** icon.
2. Tap the print with the desired combo.
3. Tap the **Change Camera Settings** icon (see Figure 5-21). The settings for that image will be activated for use with the camera.
4. Return to the camera back, and snap your image.
5. Over time, you may find you have a bunch of Hipstamatic combos you want to preserve (see Figure 5-32).

FIGURE 5-32: *The grunge frame and off-kilter colors of the image on the left were produced with the Lucifer VI lens and the Kodot Verichrome film. In the center image, the saturated colors and vintage frame were created by choosing the John S Lens and Pistil film. The somewhat muted colors of the image on the right were produced with the Kaimal Mark II Lens, the Float film, and the Cadet Blue Gel flash.*

Re-creating the Darkroom Experience

Serious photographers, both pros and amateurs, once took enormous pride in printing their own images. The darkroom was where photos came alive, and to have the chops to call yourself a bona fide photographer, you needed to spend hours upon hours in the darkroom, perfecting your craft. That was then, this is now, and now the darkroom is about as much a relic of a bygone era as eight-track tapes and dial telephones.

Of course, its status as a relic certainly constitutes a big part of the darkroom's allure and fascination, often among people who never set foot in a darkroom (and never will). So, what is a darkroom, and what did people do in there? Here's a quick rundown to help you understand the tools and terminology used by apps meant to reproduce the darkroom experience:

▶ **Film processing**   Film needs to be processed with chemicals in order to convert it into negatives (or, in the case of slides, positive images). The negative images would then be ready for printing.

▶ **Enlarger**   An enlarger is a device with a lens to project a negative image onto photographic paper, which is placed in an easel to hold the paper.

▶ **Paper**   Photographic paper is specially coated, light-sensitive paper.

▶ **Chemicals**   To process the paper, a series of chemical solutions would be laid out in trays. A typical process included four trays, for developer, stop bath, fixer, and wash.

All of this could be rather messy, especially if it were your own darkroom and you had to mix your own chemicals. That's the fun of these darkroom apps. They're something of a game. You get to play darkroom, as it were, without ever having to do the cleanup.

The Fantasy Darkroom World of SwankoLab

Hipstamatic is terrific fun, but it has a downside: You can't use it to process photos you've already taken with your iPhone camera. For that, there's another app, SwankoLab (Synthetic Corp.; $1.99), from the company behind Hipstamatic, and it's a joy-inducing ride into photographic nostalgia. Like Hipstamatic, SwankoLab is an app that's lots of fun, with a premium on style. In fact, as you enter the world of SwankoLab, you might feel like you're playing a game rather than processing photos. That's because SwankoLab essentially turns the darkroom experience into a funhouse world in the form of an iPhone app. It's wildly fun, it's strange, and it's beautiful, and it produces wonderful images with a tool whose game-like qualities mask a lot of image-editing brawn and potential (see Figure 5-33).

To get started, follow these steps:

1. Open the app, and then load an image, as instructed.
2. After an image is loaded, you will be transported, funhouse-style, into the wholesale darkroom experience, courtesy of SwankoLab, as shown in Figure 5-34. If you've been in a darkroom, SwankoLab's version of a darkroom will seem strangely and amusingly familiar (and just slightly

askew)—the chemicals on the shelf, the beaker, the trays, the timer, the safe-light. You can just about smell the fixer stinging your nostrils. If you've never set foot in a darkroom, then here's your chance to pretend you're reliving an experience you never had.

FIGURE 5-33: *An image processed with SwankoLab*

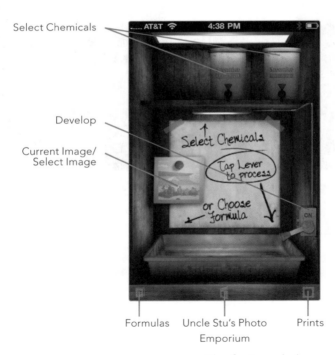

FIGURE 5-34: *The fantasy dark-room look of SwankoLab*

3. See those chemicals arrayed on the shelf? You'll use those to process your image. Flick among them to check them out. SwankoLab helpfully displays a description of each one. Grizzle Fix, for instance, will produce "ultra-aged" prints, while Swanko A19 Developer will produce prints with a "warm burn and oversaturation." Each chemical is assigned a number of units; you can add up to eight units of chemicals for each print.

4. When you want to add a chemical, tap it, and you will see it descend and spill the chemicals into a tray, as shown in Figure 5-35. Add more chemicals.

5. Tap **On** to process your image. Your image will slide into a tray, and you'll see a darkroom timer count down the seconds.

6. You will then see your image hanging up to dry (see Figure 5-36).

7. Tap **Save** to save your image.

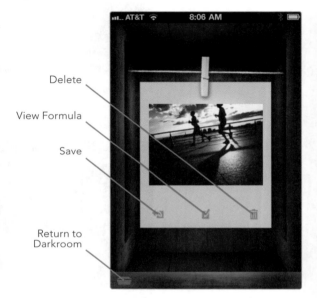

Delete

View Formula

Save

Return to Darkroom

FIGURE 5-35: *Adding chemicals to the darkroom tray before processing an image*

FIGURE 5-36: *An image hanging up to dry in SwankoLab*

All of this would make for an amusing darkroom experience, but there's more. SwankoLab allows you to use ready-made "formulas" of chemicals available when you purchase the app. In addition, you can create your own formulas and even preserve notes about what those formulas do. These features turn Swanko-Lab into a tool with advanced capabilities for creating your own custom effects. Here's how:

1. From the print drying screen (see Figure 5-36), tap the **View Formula** icon.

2. SwankoLab displays the chemicals used. It also includes fields to name your formula and jot down notes about it, as shown in Figure 5-37. If you want to preserve a formula for future use, enter that information, and then tap **Save**.

3. The Saved Formulas screen appears. You can now use your formula by tapping it.

To use formulas in the future, including the ready-made formulas you get with the app, follow these steps:

1. Tap the **Formulas** icon from the darkroom screen. The list of available formulas appears, as shown in Figure 5-38.

2. Tap the formula, and then tap **Use Formula** when prompted. You can also tap the blue arrow (see Figure 5-38) to inspect the chemicals used in the formula.

3. Proceed to print by tapping the **On** button.

FIGURE 5-37: *Creating a custom formula in SwankoLab*

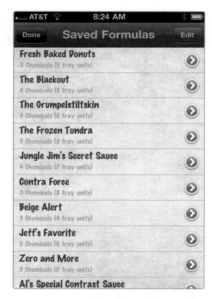

FIGURE 5-38: *The formulas available in SwankoLab, including custom formulas*

Just as with Hipstamatic, you're able to make additional purchases within the app. For $1.99, you can subscribe to the darkroom supply catalog for Uncle Stu's Photo Emporium. That gives you a lifetime subscription, which means you get additional chemicals—the ones in the current catalog—as well as any chemicals introduced in the future. It's a bargain and certainly worth it for such a wonderful app.

CameraKit

With CameraKit (Tetsuya Chiba; $1.99), you "develop" your photos by adjusting settings from the Develop button. You can make the following adjustments by opening the app and then tapping **Develop** before you have loaded or snapped a photo (as shown in Figure 5-39):

► **Film**   These will "print" your image as a color photo, black-and-white, sepia, or classic (with a high-contrast color look).

► **Soft Focus**   Add a soft focus look by setting this to Lv.1 (minimal) to Lv.3 (strong).

► **Cross Processing**   This gives your image a cross-processed look, similar to those available with the Cross Process app.

► **Push/Pull Processing**   When developing film, photographers would sometimes expose the film to chemicals for less (or more) time and at a different temperature in order to generate a certain effect or compensate for a camera's exposure problems (or a photographer's mistakes in adjusting camera settings). In this app, the negative numbers will generate an overexposed (lighter) image, while the positive number will produce an underexposed (darker) image.

► **Flash and Vignette**   You're also able to add a vignette effect or reproduce the look of flash lighting by turning those settings to **On**.

Once you have your settings, just tap the camera icon to snap a photo or the load photo icon to load an image from your iPhone photos. Tap **Save** to save your image (see Figure 5-40).

FIGURE 5-39: You can tap Develop to view CameraKit's settings to "develop" your image.

FIGURE 5-40: An image processed with CameraKit, using the Classic setting, vignetting set to On, and push/pull processing set to +1

Use Cross Process to Create Beautiful Mistakes

You know the look when you see it—strangely unnatural colors, lots of contrast, and sometimes an otherworldly bluish tint. That's the look (well, really just one of the looks) typical of *cross processing*, which is the photographic technique of processing one type of film in chemicals meant for another type of film. Photographers likely stumbled on this technique when using the wrong chemicals during a sleep-deprived (or otherwise impaired) state. Yes, you got it right: Here's an app that mimics mistakes, though these are mistakes loved by photographers.

To use Cross Process (Nick Campbell; $0.99), follow these steps:

1. Open the app, and then tap **Cancel** (yes, this isn't quite the most intuitive process, but this is an app about doing things the wrong way).
2. Tap the **i** button to decide how you want to cross process your image. You'll need to experiment with different effects, but setting Blue to **On** produces lovely images (see Figure 5-41). Tap **Done**.
3. Tap 📷 to snap a new image, or tap **Cancel** and then load an image by tapping the overlapping rectangles. Now you get to watch in awe as your image is processed before your eyes. It is saved automatically in your Camera Roll. The resulting image may look like a mistake, but it may be a beautiful mistake (see Figure 5-42).

FIGURE 5-41: Setting the type of process with Cross Process

FIGURE 5-42: An image produced with the Blue process set to On

Messing Up Your Pristine Images with Pic Grunger

As its name suggests, Pic Grunger (Stephen Spring; $0.99) doesn't mess around with fancy language. You want grunge, and you want it now. Well, with Pic Grunger, you've got all of those grunge photo effects you've come to know and love. To use the app, follow these steps:

1. After you open the app, tap **Resolution**—a welcome touch, because many apps hide this—to set your resolution, and then tap **Start** to select a grunge-worthy photo (see Figure 5-43).

2. Scroll through the thumbnails displaying effects, as shown in Figure 5-44, which include Acid, Aged, Blotched, Creased, Sponged, and Weathered. Select an effect.

FIGURE 5-43: *Pic Grunger puts its resolution settings front and center.*

FIGURE 5-44: *You can view thumbnails of Pic Grunger's effects.*

3. From the preview screen (see Figure 5-45), tap **Style** to experiment with different styles with fun-sounding names, such as Gig, Studio, Palooza, Back Stage, and After Hours.

4. Tap **Strength**, and use the slider to adjust the strength of the effect.

5. Tap **Border** to turn the border to On or Off.

6. Tap **Save** to save your image, which should be suitably grunged up, as shown in Figure 5-46.

FIGURE 5-45: *Tap Style to try different styles of the effect.*

FIGURE 5-46: *An image with the Weathered effect and the Gig style*

Black-and-White Images

Transform an image from color to black-and-white, and you have an instant work of art, right? Well, it's not quite that easy, but black-and-white photography certainly conjures a certain mood, whether that's the look of noir films, the feel of 1960s fashion photography, or the work of Ansel Adams or Henri Cartier-Bresson. Many apps are able to generate black-and-white images. The monochrome effects in the following apps are particularly notable and worth exploring:

▶ **CameraBag**   Use the Mono and 1962 filters.

▶ **Photo fx**   Navigate to Grads/Tints ▸ Old Photo for one batch of effects, or use Image ▸ Black and White for another batch.

▶ **PictureShow**   View the app's Noir and DuoTone effects.

Other apps specialize in black-and-white images. These apps let you explore the variety of monochrome styles used by photographers over the years, such as sepia tones and high-contrast black-and-white images.

 ## OldCamera

OldCamera (Art & Mobile; $0.99) lets you experiment with several different black-and-white looks, though it only lets you snap images, rather than process ones you've already taken. Here's how it works:

1. To choose what effect you want, open the app, and then tap **Cancel**.
2. Tap the gear icon to view the app's settings.

3. Tap **Mode**, and then select from the options (see Figure 5-47).
4. Tap **Setting** and then **Done** to preserve your changes.
5. Tap the camera icon, and you're ready to snap your image by tapping . The image will be saved to the Camera Roll (see Figure 5-48).

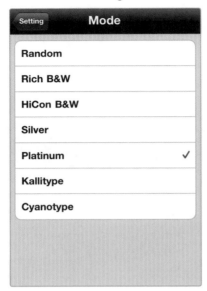

FIGURE 5-47: The monochrome effects available with OldCamera

FIGURE 5-48: An image captured with OldCamera

 ## Spica

Spica (Daisuke Nogami; $0.99) produces what it calls "super-monochrome" images—high-contrast shots with the midtones blown out into black and white (see Figure 5-49). To use the app, just open it, and then tap to take a shot. If you prefer to grab an image from your Camera Roll or Photo Library, tap **Cancel**, and then tap the overlapping photo icons to load an image. Tap the disk icon to save the image.

MonoPhix

MonoPhix (UIC Phoenxsoftware; $0.99) gives you three looks for processing your

FIGURE 5-49: A high-contrast photo from Spica

photos: Sepia (for a sepia tone), Mono (traditional black-and-white), and Antique (a rich monochrome look), as shown in Figure 5-50. It also lets you make adjustments to the default filters for each of these. Here's how:

1. After you load the app, tap **Open** to select an image.

2. Next select Sepia, Mono, or Antique (see Figure 5-51). Here we have selected Antique. Use the sliders to adjust the intensity for the light or dark shades in your image, as shown in Figure 5-52. Tap **Maximum** or **Minimum** to view the maximum or minimum effects from the filter. You can also tap **Default** to return to the default settings or **No Depth** to view the effect without a lot of contrast added or reduced.

3. Tap **Apply** to apply the filter. To undo, tap **Return**.

4. Tap **Save** to save your image to the Camera Roll.

FIGURE 5-50: *An image with the Antique filter applied*

FIGURE 5-51: *Choosing a filter in MonoPhix*

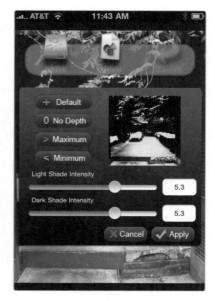

FIGURE 5-52: *Adjusting an image with MonoPhix's controls*

Vint B&W

Apps don't get much simpler than this. You open Vint B&W (Erik Pettersson; free), tap ⬛, and you've got your black-and-white photo (see Figure 5-53).

FIGURE 5-53: *A photo snapped with Vint B&W*

Resurrecting Films of the Past with Film Lab

When buying film, photographers once could choose from among a staggering number of options. These options included not only numerous brands, such as Agfa, Fuji, and Kodak, but also the varied mix of films made by those companies. Each film was known for particular characteristics—a high-contrast look for this one, lots of graininess for that one, and on and on. Film Lab (CLBITZ Ubiquitous Communications; $0.99) resurrects these films in the form of an iPhone app that lets you apply filters to summon the look of scores of photographic films.

To use Film Lab, follow these steps:

1. Open the app, and then tap the **Load/Save** icon to load your image, as shown in Figure 5-54.
2. Tap the **Film Simulation** icon, which is your route to the app's filters. The app provides options for sorting through and viewing these filters (as shown in Figure 5-55):

    ▶ **Film Brand** The app's simulated films separated into film brands, such as Kodak, Polaroid, and others (see Figure 5-56)

    ▶ **Vintage** Films with a vintage look

    ▶ **Sepia** Films providing a sepia tone

Settings

Editing Tools

Film Simulation

Redo

Undo

Load/Save

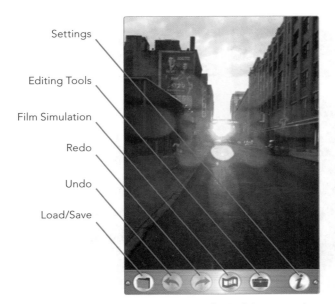

FIGURE 5-54: *Film Lab's controls*

FIGURE 5-55: *The options available from the Film Simulation icon*

▸ **All Films** A list of all available films in Film Lab

▸ **Others** Films separated into categories such as B&W, Color, Cross Processing, Fade, and Warm

▸ **Recent** Filters you have recently applied

▸ **Favorite** Any films marked as your favorites

3. From any of those options, tap a particular company, era, or look, and the app will display thumbnails of the available films. Tap each of these to see a preview, with the film's name and details displayed on your image temporarily (as shown in Figure 5-57). If you want to label a particular film as a favorite, for easy access later, tap the star icon.

4. To apply a filter, tap **OK**.

5. To make additional image adjustments for brightness/contrast, hue/saturation, color, and sharpness, tap **Editing Tools**.

6. To save your image, tap **Load/Save**, and then tap **Save**.

Are the results from Film Lab truly authentic? That's debatable. It's certainly a fun journey into photographic history, if not an entirely reliable one.

FIGURE 5-56: *Reviewing the Film Brand options*

FIGURE 5-57: *You can review the effects from various film filters.*

From App to the Desktop

Once you use a streamlined, wonderfully intuitive tool like CameraBag or Pic Grunger to re-create the beautiful look of old-time photos, you may not want to go back to the laborious work required to edit your photos in Photoshop or similarly complex desktop photo-editing tools. Couldn't you just have those tools on your laptop or desktop computer, too? In fact, you can—sort of. Consider this one more way the popularity of Apple's apps is influencing the software world. Rather than a program (or brand) starting out as desktop software (as in the case of Photoshop) and then making its way onto the iPhone as an app, now software is going in the opposite direction, too, from an app available in the App Store to a program available for your computer. That's just what's happened with CameraBag. The app is now available as desktop software for Macintosh and Windows, with its creator marketing the app for its simplicity: "CameraBag recreates the magic of film in a fast, intuitive, minimal interface: choose a photo, choose a filter, and you're done." Expect more app-like features in your photo-editing software in the future. Photoshop has its place, no doubt, but for much of our image editing, we don't want lots of menus and palettes cramming our screen. We want simplicity, fun, and the chance to experiment, and CameraBag delivers just that. That retro look you love? You can have it on your desktop, too.

6

Fun and Offbeat Effects

Photographic experimentation takes lots of forms. Sometimes you want to create an intricately detailed artwork with the help of retouching brushes, filters, and sundry other tools. Other times you want to see what your brother's head would look like on your dog's body. Photography is many things to many people, and with the iPhone, it's often source material for the latest laugh-out-loud email that makes the rounds among you and your buddies. An entire category of photography apps is devoted to amusing yourself (and others) with your iPhone camera, whether by creating comic strips or producing 3D images with your iPhone photos. Your iPhone camera is something of a multipurpose funhouse machine. With the help of a variety of apps, you can turn it into a plastic toy camera, an arcade photo booth, and a creator of off-the-wall artwork. Whatever apps you use, they'll keep you occupied for hours.

Toy Cameras

The term *toy camera* typically refers to cheap cameras made out of plastic, like the Diana-F and the Lomo LC-A. But the name is something of a misnomer. These cameras have earned a following among a mix of hipsters and artists for their sometimes unexpectedly beautiful results, often from light leaking onto the film. Though cheap, they weren't really meant as toys—they require 35mm film—and collectors and film fans continue to use them; modern-art museums even stock these "toy cameras" in their gift shops. It's no surprise, then, to find toy cameras, or digital versions of them, showing up as iPhone apps. These apps typically try to replicate the appealing imperfections common among toy camera photos. Their capabilities vary from app to app, and some of them attempt to re-create the toy camera experience with special "films" and plastic-looking camera controls.

Plastic Bullet

Snap a photo with Plastic Bullet (Red Giant Software; $1.99), and you can just about make anything look beautiful. Light leaks and ethereal colors abound in the app's effects. Plastic Bullet lets you snap photos or give a toy camera look to images in your Camera Roll and Photo Library. After you review Plastic Bullet's handiwork, tap the **Refresh** button (see Figure 6-1), and you'll see additional variations of your photos. You can keep tapping forever for infinite effects. Just be sure to tap the heart icon to save your image of choice to the Camera Roll (see Figure 6-2).

Refresh

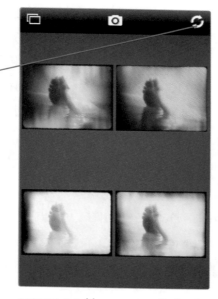

FIGURE 6-1: *You can tap Refresh to view additional variations.*

FIGURE 6-2: *An image processed with Plastic Bullet*

CAMERAtan

Here's a toy camera app with a truly toylike feel. After you load an image with CAMERAtan (MorokoshiMan; $0.99), you're able to choose from effects represented by stickerlike symbols, as shown in Figure 6-3. Under Effect Level, tap **−1** or **−2** to decrease the strength of the effect. And because you can apply multiple effects just by tapping **Add Processing** (see Figure 6-4), CAMERAtan doubles as a sophisticated tool to alter your iPhone photos.

FIGURE 6-3: *Choosing an effect with CAMERAtan*

FIGURE 6-4: *You can tap Add Processing to add an additional effect.*

 ## Andigraf

Andigraf (Subkernel; $1.99) packs a lot of features into a toy camera. Open this multishot camera, and you can play with the Adjust Interval dial to tell Andigraf how much time you want between shots, as shown in Figure 6-5. Tap **Change Lens/Film**, and you can flick among different lenses (see Figure 6-6) and film types (Figure 6-7). All of this makes for a decidedly fun experience, with results to match.

 * **NOTE: Do you love toy cameras? Then consider exploring some of the others available at the App Store, including ClassicSAMP, ClassicTOY, QuadCamera, and ToyCamera.**

View Photos

Adjust Interval

Take Photo

Change Lens and Film

FIGURE 6-5: Andigraf gives you options for capturing multishot images.

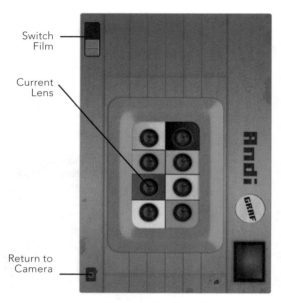

Switch Film

Current Lens

Return to Camera

FIGURE 6-6: Andigraf includes a variety of lenses to let you capture four, eight, or nine shots per Andigraf composition.

Photo Booths

Did people have more fun in the olden days, or what? That's the conceit, or part of it, of photo booth apps. How couldn't you have a fun time stuffing yourself (and your friends) into a cramped booth and going wild? Now you can do this without the photo booth or time travel.

IncrediBooth

This app is made for the front-facing camera of the iPhone 4. With Incredi-Booth (Synthetic Corp.; $0.99), you stare at yourself on the iPhone screen and then press the app's big red shutter button (see Figure 6-8) when you want to start snapping a series of four images; if you like, you can adjust the effects generated by IncrediBooth by "turning" the dial surrounding the shutter button. To view the

FIGURE 6-7: Flick to choose different films, including LoMode Turquoise, 1945S Classic Sepia Tone, and Graf Photo.

results, tap the **Photos Outside** arrow, and view your recent photo booth strips (see Figure 6-9). To save one to the Camera Roll (or share it), tap the strip, and then tap **Share** (see Figure 6-10).

FIGURE 6-8: *Tap the shutter button to start snapping images, or adjust the dial for different effects.*

FIGURE 6-9: *You're able to review your recent photo booth strips.*

 ## Photo Booth Classic Plus

With Photo Booth Classic Plus (Vurb Studio; $1.99), you have the option to take your photos in true photo booth style, or you can simply choose them from your existing iPhone photos. Either way, the app cobbles these together in a fun photo booth strip. To take a traditional photo booth strip, just tap **Take Pics** and watch as a countdown begins to prepare you to smile, grimace, or whatever. Tap the clock button in the upper-right corner (see Figure 6-11), and you can adjust the time between shots, with custom settings from

FIGURE 6-10: *You can tap Share to share your image or save it.*

1 second to 60 seconds. If you would rather assemble a photo booth strip from your iPhone photos, tap **Select Pics**, and then choose the four images from your Camera Roll; the app lets you resize each one after it's loaded. Once your strip is ready, you're able to adjust the color (or turn it into a black-and-white strip), as shown in Figure 6-12. Tap **Publish** to save your strip or share it.

FIGURE 6-11: *You're able to adjust the number of seconds between shots.*

FIGURE 6-12: *Adjust your photo booth strip once it's ready, or save or share it.*

Multiframe Constructions with Diptic

iPhone photography apps often let you create something wonderful with a minimal amount of work. Diptic (Peak Systems; $1.99) is different. The app's interface is straightforward, but it's about combining multiple photos (or pieces of them) into a single image (see Figure 6-13), and that requires a fair amount of planning. Before firing up Diptic, you may want to edit your images in other apps and decide on their placement in your multiframe composition. Once you start placing your images within

FIGURE 6-13: *An image created with Diptic*

Diptic, you may realize the individual frames—some square, others elongated rectangles—require some unusual cropping of your photos. All of this can be wonderfully creative. Just don't think you'll have a winner of an image without thinking through what you want to accomplish.

To use Diptic, follow these steps:

1. Open the app, and then flick through the layouts to review them (see Figure 6-14). Tap a layout to select it.
2. Once you have selected a layout, tap a frame to select an image to place there. Once an image is inside a frame, you're able to drag and zoom to position it inside the frame. Add additional images until your composition is complete.
3. Tap **Effects** to adjust the brightness, contrast, or colors in an image, as shown in Figure 6-15.
4. Tap **Border** to alter the frame border (see Figure 6-16). The top slider controls the width of the border. Tap Black or White for a border with those colors, or use the red, green, and blue sliders to create a custom color for your border.
5. To finalize your image, tap **Export**, and then tap To Photos or To Email.

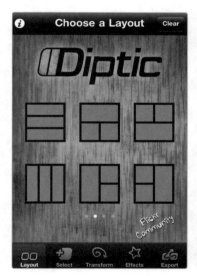

FIGURE 6-14: *Reviewing the available layouts in Diptic*

FIGURE 6-15: *You can adjust the brightness, contrast, and colors of individual frames in Diptic.*

FIGURE 6-16: *Making adjustments to the frame border*

Selective Color with Color Splash

Remember *The Wizard of Oz*, with its brilliant blast of color when Dorothy finds herself in Oz? Color was once special in photography (and film), and now it's just what we expect; we're often immune to its joys. Color Splash (Pocket Pixels; $1.99) is an antidote to this. Using a technique known as *selective desaturation* for the way it removes the color for all but one portion of an image, you can produce a photograph with brilliant colors drawing attention to your subject. Follow these steps:

1. Open the app, and load an image. The image is automatically converted to a black-and-white photo, as shown in Figure 6-17.
2. By tapping **Pan & Zoom**, you're able to zoom into the area of the image you want to colorize without accidentally "painting" on the image.
3. Tap **Color**, and then, using your finger, paint a portion of the photo to add color back to the image (see Figure 6-18). You can also zoom when Color is selected, using the two-finger pinch-and-spread technique, but you may find yourself accidentally painting color onto your image when trying to zoom.

Menu —

Brushes —

Undo —

FIGURE 6-17: *When you load an image into Color Splash, it is converted to black and white.*

FIGURE 6-18: *Use a finger to "paint" over the area you want colorized. The photo's original colors will reappear.*

4. Toggle between Pan & Zoom and Color in order to zoom down to the pixel level to make detailed adjustments, especially around the edges of the colorized area. If you want to view the precise area that's been colorized, tap the red dot. A red "mask" appears over the colorized portion of the image, making it easy to see whether you have missed any crucial pieces. No red is added to your image; the mask is simply a visualization of the colorized area.

5. Tap the **Menu** icon and then **Save Image** to save the image to your Camera Roll (see Figure 6-19).

Once you experiment with Color Splash, you may also want to consider adjusting its brush sizes and types. Tap the **Menu** icon and then **Settings**; set the Brush Size slider to **On**. That will allow you to determine the size of the brush and choose among transparent and opaque brushes (as shown in Figure 6-20). With the transparent brushes, color is added incrementally as you paint over an area rather than completely restored, as happens with the opaque brushes.

Transparent Brushes

Opaque Brushes

FIGURE 6-19: *An image edited with Color Splash (PHOTO CREDIT: Dianne Rosky)*

FIGURE 6-20: *Color Splash lets you choose brush sizes and types.*

3D Photos with 3D Camera

3D is all the rage, and now you can create your own three-dimensional photos with your iPhone. With 3D Camera (Juicy Bits; $1.99), you take two photos with your iPhone, one after another, and then align them to create a 3D anaglyph—an image made up of two superimposed layers to create the effect of depth when viewed through special glasses. Here's how:

1. Open the app, and then compose your initial (left) image. Tap 📷.
2. Without moving the camera up or down, shift the camera to the right, and then take your second (right) image. And how much should you shift the camera to the right? In general, you want to shift 1/30th of the distance to the subject of your photo, or about 3 inches if your subject is 8 feet away from you.
3. The app displays one image superimposed over the other. Drag a finger across your iPhone screen to align the images, as shown in Figure 6-21. By touching and holding one spot on your screen, you're able to magnify that area to align the images precisely.

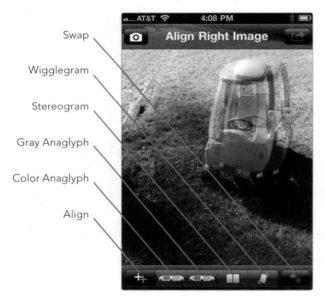

Swap
Wigglegram
Stereogram
Gray Anaglyph
Color Anaglyph
Align

FIGURE 6-21: *A 3D image being created*

4. When you're satisfied with the alignment, tap the **Color Anaglyph** icon to produce the anaglyph. You can also try other 3D methods, including Gray Anaglyph, Stereogram, and Wigglegram, but the Color Anaglyph is usually the most satisfying option. If you decide you want to realign your image, tap the **Align** button, and you can try again.

5. Tap ⬆ to save or share your image.

Diehard 3D fans may want to investigate the app's settings. Tap the iPhone's Settings app, and then **3D Camera**. You're able to alter the image size and experiment with alternative methods for representing the colors in the 3D anaglyph. Whatever the case, you will need 3D glasses to view your image. Visit *http://www .juicybitssoftware.com/faq/* for tips on where to buy them (or get free ones).

Build a LEGO Construction with LEGO Photo

Want to see your face as a LEGO construction? LEGO Photo (The LEGO Group; free) lets you do just that. Just be sure to select an image with big, obvious details. Close-ups generally work a lot better than nature scenes or other distance shots. Here's how this works:

1. Open the app, and then take a new photo or upload an existing one.
2. Tap the finger icon to watch the LEGO tiles morph into your image. Swipe across the screen to view your image with different color combinations.
3. Tap the **i** icon (see Figure 6-22), and then tap **Save** to save your image. Hold the image at arm's length to view it.

FIGURE 6-22: *LEGO Photo lets you convert your images into LEGO artworks.*

Comic Strips with Strip Designer

Strip Designer (Vivid Apps; $2.99) lets you create comic strips right on your iPhone, using your iPhone photos. You choose a layout for your strip, select your photos, and add speech balloons. Here's how:

1. Open the app, and then tap **New Strip**.
2. Choose a layout category and then the template (as shown in Figure 6-23).

3. From the template, add your photos by tapping the frames within the layout and choosing images. Use one finger to move a photo within the frame. Use two fingers to enlarge or rotate it.

4. Tap any photo to access tools for editing your image, as shown in Figure 6-24. These allow you to apply a sepia tone, turn your image into a sketch, add contrast, and make other adjustments.

5. Tap **Done** when you have finished adjusting your images.

6. To add a speech balloon or sticker as well as text, tap **Add**, and then tap **Balloon** or **Sticker** (see Figure 6-25). You're able to drag these around the screen to position them.

7. Tap **Share** to save the strip or share it (see Figure 6-26).

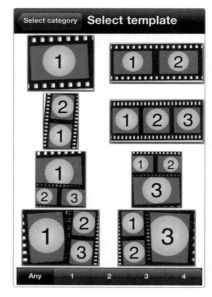

FIGURE 6-23: *Choosing a template for a comic strip*

FIGURE 6-24: *Strip Designer provides tools to edit individual images within your comic strip.*

FIGURE 6-25: *You can create and position speech bubbles with the app.*

FIGURE 6-26: *A comic strip panel created with Strip Designer*

Monet and Picasso, via ArtCamera

ArtCamera (MacPhun; $0.99) applies filters to mimic the styles of famous artists and art periods. Here's how to generate your masterpiece:

1. Load your photo, and then tap the **Filters** icon (see Figure 6-27).
2. Tap **Art** from the available categories.
3. Review the filter choices, which include Art Poster, Claude Monet, Neon Light, Pablo Picasso, and others. Tap your choice.
4. Tap **Apply** to apply the filter to your image.
5. Tap **Save** to save your image or share it.

The app includes other filters, too, including ones to invert your image, add contrast, or give your photo a burned or crumpled paper look. For these, tap **Additional** (rather than Art) after you select the Filters icon.

FIGURE 6-27: *The Claude Monet filter was applied to this image.*

Ransom-Note Lettering with Ransom Letters

Cut-out magazine lettering has a fun, do-it-yourself appeal, and you can avoid the glue and the scissors with Ransom Letters (More Blu Sky; $0.99), an app for overlaying your photos with a message written with ransom-style lettering. Follow these steps:

1. Open the app, and then tap the **Take It** icon to load a photo from your camera or iPhone photo albums (see Figure 6-28).
2. Tap **Type It**, and then enter your message. Tap **Done**.
3. After the letters appear, you're able to drag each word around the screen (see Figure 6-29). You can also randomly choose different letter styles by shaking your phone. Pinch your thumb and forefinger together over a word to make it bigger or smaller.
4. Tap **Ransom** to view the menu again, and then tap **Save It** to save your image or share it.

Digital Glitches and Off-the-Wall Artworks with Satromizer

To create a one-of-a-kind digital artwork, with odd glitches and color artifacts, experiment with Satromizer (Ben Syverson; $2.99), an app named after Jon Satrom, a new media artist who often employs glitches in his artwork. To use Satromizer, follow these steps:

1. After you open the app, tap the **i** icon.

FIGURE 6-28: Use the Take It icon to load a photo into the app.

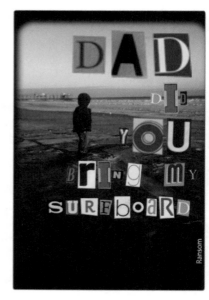

FIGURE 6-29: You can position words by dragging them around the screen.

2. Next adjust the slider to the left or right, as shown in Figure 6-30, if you want the illusion of having some degree of control with the effects generated by Satromizer.

3. Tap the broken file icon to load an image.

4. Now drag your finger across the your photo to generate random effects.

5. Tap the **i** icon again and then the disc icon with the question mark to save your image to your Camera Roll. Your photo will likely be unrecognizable, as shown in Figure 6-31.

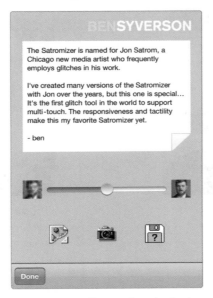

FIGURE 6-30: *Satromizer includes rather nontraditional-looking controls.*

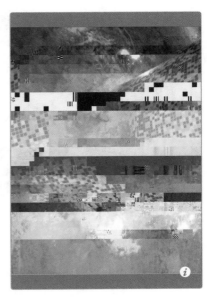

FIGURE 6-31: *An image run through the Satromizer app*

Graphic Novel Sketches with ToonPAINT

Load an image into ToonPAINT (Toon-FX; $1.99), and seconds later you'll be going gaga about a sketch generated from your photo in the style of a hip graphic novel (see Figure 6-32). ToonPAINT's automatic results are often all you'll want, but if you decide you want make adjustments, you can do that, too (see Figure 6-33):

▶ **Edges/Gray/Black** You can tap this icon to view sliders for adjusting the strength of the edges, as well as the amount of gray and black in your sketch.

▶ **Advanced** From the Edges/Gray/Black icon, you can tap Advanced for additional settings to experiment with the automatic sketch generated by ToonPAINT. In general, selecting L or XL from the settings for Coherence, Edge Width, or Edge Length will distort your image, sometimes in fun and unexpected ways.

▶ **Paint** You can tap the Paint icon for a brush to add colors by painting on your sketch. You're able to select both the colors to add and the brush size.

FIGURE 6-32: *That's me near the Brooklyn Bridge, via ToonPAINT.*

Save

Paint

Edges/
Gray/Black

Load
Image

FIGURE 6-33: *You can make adjustments to the sketch generated in ToonPAINT.*

Photo Mashups with Juxtaposer

Ever wonder what your head would look like on your cat's body? Now is your chance to find out. You can use Juxtaposer (Pocket Pixels; $2.99) to superimpose an element from one image, like a face, on another image. The controls of the app work the same way as those in Color Splash, which is made by the same company. Follow these steps to generate your juxtaposed image:

1. Open Juxtaposer, and then load your "base" image. You will add elements from another image (or more than one image) onto that one.
2. After you load your base image, the app asks you to choose an image for the elements to be added. It then places a smaller version of that image atop the base image (as shown in Figure 6-34). You will be erasing portions of that "top image" until only the portion you want to superimpose on the base image remains.
3. Tap **Move Top Image** to move it into the right position. You're able to zoom in and out and drag it around the screen.
4. As in Color Splash, you toggle between the Pan & Zoom and Erase tools to work with your image, erasing portions of the top image to achieve the desired effect (see Figure 6-35).

5. Tap the **Menu** icon and then **Save Image** to save the image to your Camera Roll.

FIGURE 6-34: *Juxtaposer places a small version of your top image atop your base image.*

FIGURE 6-35: *Erasing the top image to blend it with another image*

A Psychedelic Look with PhotoTropedelic

The artist Peter Max's psychedelic style was everywhere in the 1960's—he appeared on the cover of *Life* in 1969—and now you can turn your photos into psychedelic-looking images with the app PhotoTropedelic (Larry Weinberg; $1.99), as shown in Figure 6-36.

FIGURE 6-36: *The original image, and one processed with PhotoTropedelic*

Here's how:

1. Open the app, and then tap the folder icon (see Figure 6-37) to select an image from your albums or snap a new one.
2. PhotoTropedelic then converts your image into a psychedelic-looking artwork.
3. You're also able to experiment with the app's settings to achieve various results (see Figure 6-38). You can increase the level of details, use additional colors, and decide whether you want to include circles, rays, and other effects in your image.
4. Once you have an image you want to preserve, tap ⬀ to save your image or share it.

FIGURE 6-37: PhotoTropedelic's controls

FIGURE 6-38: PhotoTropedelic lets you experiment with various settings.

Share the Love (and Laughs)

After you have created that cartoon sketch or comic strip, what do you do? Just let the image sit there in your iPhone's Camera Roll? Certainly not. You want to share it. And although these apps typically let you do just that, with options for emailing your handiwork to friends or posting to Twitter, that's really just a hint of what's possible when you decide you want to start seeing what others think of your iPhone images. Sharing is a big part of the iPhone photography experience, and you have lots of ways to do just that, whether through your Flickr photostream or a photoblog.

7 Snap— and Share

After you take a photo you love, what do you do with it? If you're like a lot of people, you send it off in an email, post it to Facebook, or tweet about it. With the iPhone, you're always just a tap or two away from sharing your photos with your best buddy, your far-flung family, and the world at large. This is a vital part of the iPhone photography experience, and it's built into just about every app. You're not required to share your iPhone photos, but if you use an iPhone—a device that's all about communication, after all—then you almost certainly will.

Sharing photos takes lots of forms, depending largely on your own social networking habits. You might just want to email an occasional image to your siblings now and then, or you might seek to formulate and perfect what you believe is a hyper-organized, methodical system for posting your images to a personal greatest-hits list of social hotspots (Facebook, Twitter, and beyond). If email is enough for you, no problem, but if you want to explore other options for sharing—and for exploring the community of iPhone photographers—then there's a whole network of tools at the confluence of photography and social networking.

Crafting Your Social Networking Strategy (or Not)

What's the secret of all those social media fanatics with their dawn-to-midnight torrent of tweets and status updates? Automated tools that make it possible to post a message once and then have it appear at multiple social media hubs. To automate your own social media experience with iPhone photography, you have essentially three options:

▶ **Use your photography apps to post to social networking sites.** Not all apps have this feature, but if they do, then enter your account information to direct your apps to post your images to Facebook and elsewhere.

▶ **Set up a blog to handle your social media posts.** Blogging tools, covered in Chapter 8, allow you to configure them to post links to your photos to Facebook, Twitter, and other sites. With this method, you can post to your photoblog and have updates posted at social media hubs automatically.

▶ **Use a specialized social media workflow tool.** Pixelpipe is a cloud-based service for posting to more than 100 destinations, and it's designed specifically for media, such as photos and video. If you want your photos everywhere, consider installing Pixelpipe (Pixelpipe; free) and then directing it to post your images to scores of social media websites, photo-sharing services, and blogging platforms.

Then again, you might not want the hassles of developing a *strategy* for sharing your iPhone photos. If you don't, don't sweat it: You're not alone in wanting to scale back on your social media obligations. However you wish to share your photos, you have plenty of choices, from postcards to photo-annotated maps.

Flickr

Flickr essentially reinvented what it means to share your photos online, turning a somewhat humdrum activity into an addictive worldwide phenomenon (see Figure 7-1). A onetime startup now owned by Yahoo!, Flickr isn't just another spot to store and manage your photo collection; it's about sharing your photos with the world—and the Flickr community. With Flickr, your uploaded images become part of your personal *photostream*—essentially a chain of your photos stored online. You can classify your images as public or private, organize them into collections (called *sets*, as shown in Figure 7-2), or join specialized groups for sharing photos. With your permission, other users can tag and comment on your photos. These features make photography a social and serendipitous activity, rather than a solitary one, and they go a long way toward creating the thriving, always-evolving subculture that is Flickr.

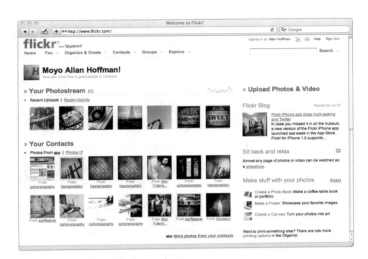

FIGURE 7-1: *The Flickr website*

FIGURE 7-2: *A Flickr user's sets, as viewed with the Flickr app*

For the uninitiated, Flickr may require a certain period of acclimation. Yet if you give Flickr a chance, you'll be rewarded with the chance to share your images with a lively and welcoming community, glean comments and tips from other iPhoneographers, and view amazing images from around the world.

* **NOTE: Flickr's free accounts are subject to a 100MB monthly photo upload limit. A "pro" account, for $24.95 a year, provides unlimited uploads and photo storage, among other perks.**

Flickr Terminology

You'll have an easier time diving into Flickr if you know the terminology:

▶ **Photostream**   These are the images you have uploaded to Flickr.

▶ **Photoset or set**   A group of images; you're able to organize your images into sets at Flickr.

▶ **Collection**   A collection is a group of your sets.

▶ **Tags**   These are terms to help categorize your photos. You're able to add tags when uploading images.

▶ **Favorite**   You can *favorite* photos taken by other people on Flickr.

▶ **Groups**   These are Flickr communities, typically organized around an interest. Popular iPhoneography-related groups include Photos Taken with an Apple iPhone, iPhoneography, iPhone 365, and Hipstamatic (see Figure 7-3).

► **Contacts** These are Flickr users whose photostreams you follow,

► **Organizr** This is Flickr's web-based tool for tagging, organizing, and otherwise managing your Flickr photos.

 The Flickr App

The Flickr app (Yahoo!; free) opens with a stunning slide show of images, using a Ken Burns effect to give a sense of motion as you're viewing photos from Flickr. To upload a photo, follow these steps:

1. Tap the camera icon from the Flickr app's home screen (shown in Figure 7-4).

2. Select **Upload from Library** to upload images from the iPhone's Photos app, and then choose your image.

FIGURE 7-3: *The Flickr iPhone-ography group, as viewed with the Flickit Pro app*

3. On the Details screen, add a title, description, and any tags, as shown in Figure 7-5. You can also decide whether to make the photo public or private. Tap **Upload** when finished.

FIGURE 7-4: *The Flickr app's simple interface*

FIGURE 7-5: *Add a title and other details to your image.*

Flickr is all about the photographic community, so it's no surprise the Flickr app helps you connect with other shutterbugs. To explore all the photos available at Flickr, use the search function from the app's home screen. You can also scan the images uploaded by your Flickr contacts and comment on their latest work:

1. Tap **Contacts** on the home screen.
2. Tap the name of the contact whose images you want to view. Your contact's page displays his photostream, as shown in Figure 7-6. If you would rather view the photographer's images by sets and tags, select **Sets & Tags**. You're also able to view images the photographer labeled as favorites.
3. Tap an image to view a particular photo. From the photo, you're able to mark it as a favorite or comment on it (see Figure 7-7).

FIGURE 7-6: *A contact's photo-stream in the Flickr app*

FIGURE 7-7: *The Flickr app lets you mark images as favorites and comment on them. (PHOTO CREDIT: Dave Keane)*

* *NOTE:* **Not a fan of Flickr? Other photo management services, such as Phanfare and Photobucket, have their own iPhone apps.**

 Flickit Pro

Really into Flickr? Then think about springing for Flickit Pro (Green Volcano Software; $4.99), a wonderful app with far more features than the official Flickr app, such as uploading in bulk, viewing photos by Flickr group (see Figure 7-8), and viewing a map of Flickr images snapped at nearby locations. It also provides some fun, eye-popping options for viewing your photos, as shown in Figure 7-9.

FIGURE 7-8: *You can view your Flickr groups from the Flickit Pro app.*

FIGURE 7-9: *Flipping through photos with Flickit Pro*

✳ **NOTE: Also consider Darkslide Premium, FlickStackr, and Mobile Fotos if you're looking for an app to make up for the limitations of the official Flickr app.**

Facebook

With the Facebook app (Facebook; free), you can easily share photos with your Facebook friends. Your photos will show up in your news feed, and your friends can "like" them, comment on them, and spread the love. To upload photos to Facebook from your iPhone, first install the Facebook app and create a photo album for storing your images. To create an album, follow these steps:

1. Tap **Photos**, as shown at the bottom of Figure 7-10.
2. Tap **+** at the top right to add a new album. If you already have photo albums at Facebook, you will see them displayed, as shown in Figure 7-11.

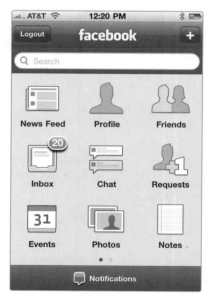

FIGURE 7-10: *The Facebook app*

3. Provide a name for your album, as well as a location and description, if desired. Tap **Create** (see Figure 7-12) to see your new album.

FIGURE 7-11: *Facebook photo albums, with the + sign used to add new albums*

FIGURE 7-12: *You're able to name your albums, as well as provide a location and description.*

To upload a photo, follow these steps:

1. You have two options to upload photos. To upload images to a specific album, tap **Photos**, and then tap the album where you want to store the image. Next tap the camera icon in the upper-right corner of the screen. To upload images right from your newsfeed, you're able to tap the camera icon, as shown in Figure 7-13; these images will be stored in your Mobile Uploads album.

2. Next choose **Take Photo** or **Choose From Library**.

3. After you've chosen your image, write a caption, if you choose, and then tap **Upload**. Your image will then appear in the newsfeed.

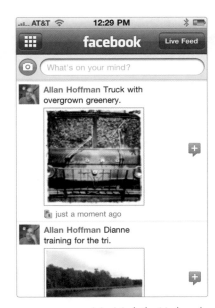

FIGURE 7-13: *My Mobile Uploads album*

You may also want to tag your images with your friends' names:

1. Tap **Photos** and then the name of the album with the image (or images) you want to tag.
2. Tap the photo to tag, and then tap 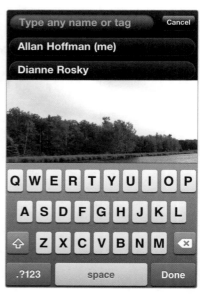, which will allow you to tag the image, as well as "like" it, make it your profile picture, or delete it, as shown in Figure 7-14. Tap **Tag This Photo**.
3. To tag a person, tap the individual in the photo, which will open a field to type in a name (see Figure 7-15). As you type the person's name in the text field, Facebook will suggest individuals. Tap the name of the person you want to tag in the photo.
4. Select **Done**.

FIGURE 7-14: *Tagging and other options*

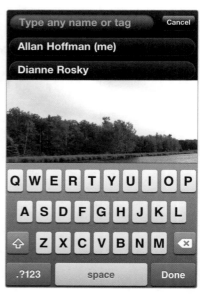

FIGURE 7-15: *You're able to type your friends' names in order to tag them within photos.*

Twitter

For a service that's all about brief, pithy messages, Twitter can sure get complicated. An entire Twitter-obsessed industry exists with apps, services, and tools to tap into the vast Twitter universe. But if you're looking to post an image to Twitter, you don't really want to deal with a gazillion choices. And you don't really need to do so. Twitter's own iPhone app, Twitter (Twitter; free), lets you post images, and it also provides flexibility in deciding where those images will be hosted. That's right: When you post an image to Twitter, you're really just posting a URL pointing to an image that's stored elsewhere.

To get started, download the Twitter app and enter your Twitter account information when prompted. The app includes a detailed manual, right within the app; to find it, tap **Settings** and then **Manual**. As for posting images, follow these steps:

1. Tap **Accounts** and then **Settings**.
2. From Settings, choose **Services**.
3. Tap **Image Service**.
4. Tap your selection, as shown in Figure 7-16. TwitPic is a popular choice.
5. After you have chosen your image-hosting service, tap **Services**, then **Settings**, and then **Done**.

Now you're ready to start posting images to Twitter. Here's how:

1. From your Twitter feed, tap the **Post** icon, as shown in Figure 7-17.
2. Next tap the Twitter app's **Action** icon (see Figure 7-18), which opens your options for posting images, among other actions. (Tap the **Action** icon again, and your keyboard will reappear.) By tapping either Camera or Photo Library, you're able to take a new photo to post or use an existing one. The Twitter app lets you post multiple images in a single tweet. Just tap the Action icon again, and then add another image. Because inserting your image is actually placing text in your post—the text for the URL—you're using up a bit of your 140-character allotment with each image.
3. To view your images or revise what you've chosen, tap the attachments button, as shown in Figure 7-19.
4. Type a message to accompany your images.
5. Tap **Send** to post your message.

FIGURE 7-16: *Choices for image hosting in the Twitter app*

FIGURE 7-17: *The Post icon is used to post images and text from the Twitter app.*

Action icon

FIGURE 7-18: *Use the Twitter app's Action icon to display the options for posting images, as well as other tools.*

FIGURE 7-19: *The attachments button lets you review the photos you're posting.*

✳ **NOTE:** If you're planning to use Posterous for a photoblog (see Chapter 8), then choose Posterous as your image service in the Twitter app.

MobileMe

MobileMe is made by Apple, and it's the only photo-sharing service that's actually built into the iPhone's Photos app. You would think this would make it the runaway favorite for photo sharing on the iPhone, but it's not; many iPhone photography buffs, for good reason, prefer Flickr and other services. MobileMe is not free, after all, and even if you have an account, the service is limited in the way it allows you to share photos from your iPhone. Even after you install the MobileMe Gallery app (Apple; free) on your iPhone, you're not able to create new photo albums from the app. For that, you need to use a web browser, such as Safari. The app's limitations and inconveniences aside, you may want to use it if you already have a boatload of photos on MobileMe and use the service with your computer.

What does the app do, then? It provides a way to view your MobileMe albums on your iPhone and share them with friends.

To share a gallery, download the app, enter your MobileMe account details, and then follow these steps:

1. Tap **My Gallery** to view your albums, as shown in Figure 7-20.
2. To share all your images, tap the envelope icon on this screen. To share a specific album, tap the album to open it, and then tap the envelope icon on the album screen.
3. An email message will open, allowing you to enter your recipients' email addresses, include a message, and then tap **Send**.

To add an image to a MobileMe album, you don't actually use the MobileMe Gallery app. For that, you use the iPhone's Photos app:

1. Tap the image to add and then . From the list, choose **Send to MobileMe**.
2. Add a title and description, if you like, and choose the album, as shown in Figure 7-21.
3. Tap **Publish**.

* **WARNING:** **Don't make things too complicated for yourself. With so many social-networking spots out there and new ones trending all the time, you could easily devote yourself to managing the social-networking side of your photographic life, only to realize you're ignoring your photography. Share your photos, sure, but don't let the sharing take over your life.**

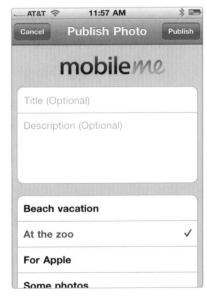

FIGURE 7-20: MobileMe albums viewed with the MobileMe Gallery app

FIGURE 7-21: From the Photos app, you're able to post to your MobileMe albums.

Sharing at Photo Printing Services

Way back when, before the advent of camera phones, the iPhone, and Flickr (when the idea of viewing photos on a screen was a novelty), online photo printing services were viewed as an innovative trend. You would have a bunch of digital images in a folder on your hard drive, upload them to Shutterfly or Snapfish, and then get prints through the mail. How cool was that? Very cool, circa 1999. And now? Been there, done that. Though photo printing services aren't exactly viewed as innovators now, these services remain immensely popular, and not just for printing images; many of them have evolved to include tools for storing images, creating slide shows, and printing holiday cards, shirts, and more. Millions of photography enthusiasts have been using these services for years and have convinced their relatives to use them, too. If that fits your profile, then you might want to stick with your choice and use these spots to share your iPhone images.

Just about all of the major photo printing services have iPhone apps:

 Gallery (Kodak Gallery; free)   This is a simple app to view your online photos, upload new images, and send emails to share your albums.

 Shutterfly (Shutterfly; free) The app connects you to your Shutterfly albums and lets you display slide shows and upload images (see Figure 7-22).

 SmugShot (SmugMug; free) This tool uploads your photos to SmugMug.

 Snapfish (Hewlett Packard; free)   View and upload your Snapfish images.

FIGURE 7-22: *The Shutterfly app*

Geotagging and Location-Based Sharing

Among the standout features of the iPhone camera is its ability to tag individual images with the location where the photo was taken. That's a powerful feature, because it enables you to use photo organization software, such as iPhoto, to sort through your photos by location. In fact, the iPhone's own Photos app lets you scan your images by location with the Places feature (see Chapter 1). Beyond the Photos app, the iPhone's location-tagging features enable a number of innovative tools for sharing photos with the help of the geographic data associated with them.

Before you use these services, you'll want to make sure you're allowing your Camera app and other iPhone photography apps to record the spots where you're snapping photos. iPhone applications are required to ask you whether you want to allow the app to use your location data, as shown in Figure 7-23. Just tap **OK** or **Don't Allow**, depending on your preferences. If OK is your answer, then you're ready to go with location-based sharing.

✳ *NOTE:* **Few cameras have the ability to tag images with location data right on the camera, for obvious reasons: Unlike the iPhone, they don't have built-in GPS chips or other location-detecting technology.**

FIGURE 7-23: A message from the Flickr app, requesting the use of location data

Location-Based iPhone Photography Apps

A number of apps—and related online services—bring together the iPhone's location-detection capabilities with the growing obsession with *check-ins* at cafes, restaurants, and clubs. After all, if you're going to say, "Here I am at McNally Jackson Books," why not do it with a photo? In fact, if you're going to go on a hike in the Rockies or a walk in Santa Monica, why not document your route with images? You can do all of that and do it right from your iPhone.

 ### EveryTrail

If you love hiking, photography, and maps—and sharing your adventures—then you'll be in nirvana with EveryTrail (GlobalMotion Media; free). Fire up the app, and you'll be able to record your route on a map as you're out on a hike (or other excursion). By taking photos along the way, your images will be pinned to locations (the abandoned stone house here, the weird tree stump there, and on and on), producing a map that has both your route and the photos you took during your hike or walk. From there, you're just a couple of taps to sharing your trip via Facebook or Twitter, where your friends will be able to view your map and photos. As a bonus, you can tap into other people's photo-documented adventures right from the app.

To set up the app's photo and sharing options, follow these steps:

1. Tap **More**, as shown in Figure 7-24.
2. Tap **Settings** and then **Picture Settings**.
3. Use the slider to choose the resolution for the photos stored within the app and uploaded to the EveryTrail website (see Figure 7-25). Be sure **Save to Camera Roll** is set to **On**. You never know when you'll take an awesome photo, and you'll want it in your Camera Roll to transfer to your computer and possibly edit with other apps.

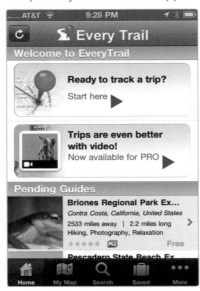

FIGURE 7-24: *The EveryTrail Home screen provides a route to the app's many options.*

FIGURE 7-25: *Use the slider to determine the photo resolution for images stored by EveryTrail. You can also choose to have your images saved to the Camera Roll.*

4. Tap **Settings** to return to the Settings screen, and then tap **Accounts for Sharing**.
5. Enter your account information for Twitter, Facebook, and YouTube—if, that is, you want to share your EveryTrail trips at those sites.
6. Tap EveryTrail's **Home** icon to return to the main app screen.

Now you're ready to document a trip:

1. Tap **My Map** and then **Start Tracking**.
2. As you proceed on your hike, bird-watching excursion, or trail run, you're able to take photos along the way, and they'll be tagged to your precise location on the route. Just tap the camera icon, as shown in Figure 7-26, to take a photo.
3. After you take your photo, you're able to decide whether to use it or do a retake. You're also able to add a caption.
4. To complete your trip, select **Details** and enter any additional information, such as the story of your trip and tips for others who follow your path.
5. Next select **Stop Tracking**, and then select **Finish and Share this Trip**.
6. Enter a title for your trip and classify your activity type from selections such as backpacking, hiking, photography, running, and snowshoeing.
7. Choose your options for sharing, as shown in Figure 7-27, and then tap **Share** to publish and share your trip.

FIGURE 7-26: *To take a photo along your route, tap the camera icon.*

FIGURE 7-27: *Before you tap the Share button, choose where you want to share your map.*

EveryTrail is a truly amazing app, with lots of possibilities for photographers. Sure, the app has *trail* in its name, and if you're an avid bird-watcher or hiker, you'll love its ability to record your every move. But even if you're not—if you're more likely to go for a walk in the city than the country—then it still has the ability to track your steps and produce a map, with photos, for you to show off to friends.

Gowalla

With Gowalla (Alamofire; free), you're able to check into locations around the world, share information about these spots with friends (or anyone else on Gowalla), and tap into rewards for your Gowalla contributions. As part of the Gowalla experience, you're able to add a photo with your check-ins. As more people add photos, Gowalla is accumulating a location-specific body of images, from cafes to national monuments.

Mopho

What's a check-in if you're not providing photographic evidence? That's the philosophy at Mopho (Happiness Engines; free), where the photo is the check-in. When you're out and about with Mopho on your iPhone, you snap an image, tag it to your location, and write a caption, and that's that—you've checked into that spot with a photo of it. Now you're part of the Mopho stream of photographic check-ins.

Pegshot

Want to let others track you by your iPhone photos? That's the idea (well, part of the idea, at least) behind Pegshot (WellcomeMat; free), which is a service for posting photos as you go about your day. After you snap an image, you're able to add a status update and decide where to share it. Pegshot will peg your shot on a map, and you're also able to choose whether you're really at the International Center of Photography, say, or the cafe around the corner.

Turning Off Geotagging

You may not want your iPhone—or particular apps—to tag your images with location data. If that's your preference, you have two choices:

▶ When using an app for the first time, choose **Don't Allow** when the app requests to use your current location.

▶ Turn off location services for all apps.

The latter option sounds simple for those who don't want location data associated with images, but it means other services—such as weather reports, movie times, and maps—won't be able to use location data, either. *Turn off location data on your iPhone with caution.* To turn off location data, perform these steps:

1. Tap the Settings app.
2. Scroll down, and tap **General**.
3. Toggle the Location Services option to **Off**.

You do have another option, if you're not sure whether you've turned location data on or off in various apps. You can tell the iPhone to reset the warnings for location services. That means all your apps using location data will ask for permission to use such data, even if you've granted an app permission previously.

Here's how to reset location warnings:

1. Tap the Settings app.
2. Scroll down, and tap **General**.
3. Select **Reset Location Warnings**.

Animoto

Want to wow your friends? Here's a surefire way to do just that. With Animoto, you're able to create fun, MTV-style videos with musical soundtracks just by uploading photos with the Animoto app (Animoto; free) right from your iPhone. "Fast, free, and shockingly easy" is how the company describes its service, and that's right. These are not typical slide shows, and they're not for control freaks—Animoto crops and adds effects to your photos—but it's a lot of fun. A basic Animoto account is free and limits you to 30-second clips, though you're able to purchase full-length videos for $3 each. If you ever need a last-minute birthday "card," assemble one with Animoto, and you'll have the recipient thinking you spent many hours on the video. Trust me, I've done this, and it works.

After you download the Animoto app, you're given the choice to sign up for an account, sign in with one you have, or just provide your email (in order for Animoto to send an email when your video is ready). After signing in, follow these steps to create your video:

1. When given the option to choose 30-second Short or Full-length Video, choose **30-second Short**, because the full-length option will cost you.

2. Next choose **Photo Library** in order to choose images to include from your photos. Select about 10 images for a 30-second video. After you have chosen your images and chosen **Continue**, the Reorder Photos screen lets you choose the order of the images by dragging them around the screen (see Figure 7-28). Select **Next** when they're in the order you'd like.

3. Next you have the chance to choose a musical selection as a soundtrack from the Genres screen. Tap a genre to view and listen to the selections. Tap a song, and then tap the **Select** button to choose your soundtrack (see Figure 7-29).

FIGURE 7-28: Drag images to reorder them.

4.   The Finalize screen lets you enter a title for your video and consider whether you want to edit your images or soundtrack, as shown in Figure 7-30. Tap **Create Video** when it's complete. Animoto will then upload the images.

5.   Your video will not be available instantaneously. It will appear under My Videos when it's ready.

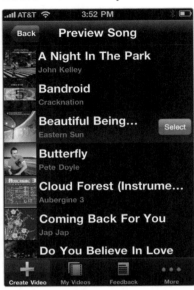

FIGURE 7-29: *You can tap Select to choose your soundtrack.*

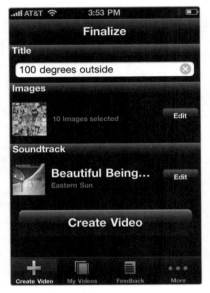

FIGURE 7-30: *Entering a title and finalizing a video*

✳ **NOTE:** The Animoto app syncs your iPhone videos with those available at the Animoto website.

Photo Postcards

Emailing photos is the most popular way to share iPhone photos, and for those occasions when you're looking for that little something extra, consider an app to let you replicate the look of a postcard. These apps let you choose one of your images as the front of the postcard and provide tools to write your message on the "back" of the card, essentially giving you a quasi-postcard experience via email.

 ### Bill Atkinson PhotoCard Lite

With Bill Atkinson PhotoCard Lite (Bill Atkinson Photography; free), you're able to fashion your own postcard by adding a photo (Figure 7-31), then typing your message, and finally applying stickers and stamps (see Figure 7-32). Your customization options vary, depending on whether you're viewing the front or the back of the card. As a bonus, you can also insert voice bubbles and then record a voice memo to accompany your email.

FIGURE 7-31: *An image for the front of the card*

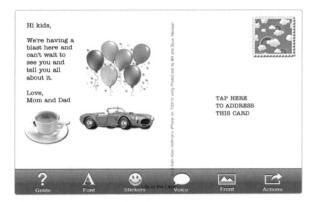

FIGURE 7-32: *When you switch to view the back of the card, you're able to type your message and apply stickers.*

Postage

Postage (RogueSheep; $4.99) has everything you expect from an iPhone app—streamlined controls, familiar icons and buttons—but with the functionality and flexibility of desktop design software targeted at consumers. The app makes it easy—and lots of fun—to create your own postcard (see Figures 7-33 and 7-34), choosing from a varied selection of appealing designs sorted into collections with labels such as love, travel, letters, holidays, and other categories. You're able to choose your photo, apply image-editing effects right from the app (sepia, black-and-white, and so forth), and adjust the fonts and colors of the text in your message. And then, of course, you can email your postcard, save it to your Camera Roll, or otherwise share it with friends.

FIGURE 7-33: *After inserting your image, you're able to apply image effects.*

FIGURE 7-34: *Postage lets you select your font and otherwise style your text.*

SodaSnap Postcards

SodaSnap Postcards (F2M2; free) produces simple postcards to email to friends (as shown in Figure 7-35). It has easy-to-understand, no-frills controls, with the resulting card putting an emphasis on your photo and your message. There's not much to learn with the app, and for a lot of occasions, that's just what you want.

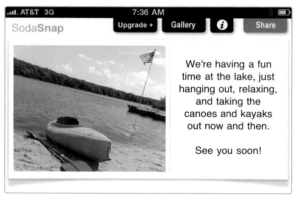

FIGURE 7-35: *A SodaSnap postcard*

Go Postal with a Postcard Sent by the USPS

As strange as it sounds, you can actually send a real postcard—just the kind your technophobic great-grandfather can hold in his hand, with a stamp on it—right from your iPhone. If the idea strikes you as a throwback, just think about the possibilities. Imagine you're on vacation in Utah—or Uganda—and you want to scribble a few postcards to your friends or parents. With these iPhone apps, you can safely shun all those gaudy postcards at trinket shops and send one of your own images. In fact, you don't even have to worry about buying a postcard and licking a stamp. You just fire up the app, choose your photo, adorn it with a border and maybe stickers, grab an address right from your contacts, and essentially say, "Please print and send this for me." Soon enough, a company located who-knows-where will print your postcard and send it off for you.

You will have to pay for this. Though the apps available for sending postcards are free, the actual postcards typically cost between $1 and $2.

 Bill Atkinson PhotoCard Lite
Cards cost two credits, with the price of the card between $1.50 and $2, depending on how many credits you buy. This is my personal favorite, with oversized postcards, stickers to apply to your message, and high-quality printing.

 goPostal (PrintYourLife.com; free) Postcards sent from the iPhone cost $1.29 with this app.

 HazelMail Postcards (HazelMail .com; free)   Cards cost $1 each when you buy prepaid HazelBucks.

 Postino (AnguriaLab; free)   You can buy one stamp to send a card for $1.99, with discounts if you buy more than one stamp at a time. The app lets you create a genuine signature for your postcards (see Figure 7-36).

FIGURE 7-36: *Use your finger to sign your postcard with Postino.*

❊ *NOTE:* **Want to send something even more retro than postcards through the mail? How about a photo booth strip? The Wink app (Shutterfly; free) lets you create and send printed photo booth strips from your iPhone. Specialized photo booth apps let you send your strips via email (see Chapter 6).**

No End to Sharing

Sharing is embedded in just about every component of the iPhoneography experience. You snap your image, and you're just a tap away from emailing it or sending it as a Multimedia Messaging Service (MMS) message. No matter how solitary an individual you are—not very, if you own an iPhone—you're going to share your iPhone photos at one time or another. It's irresistible. You snap an image, you like it, and you want someone else to share your sense of wonder. Just remember, it's up to you to decide whether you go all-out, posting at Twitter and Facebook and scores of other spots, or whether you want to foster connections at your own quiet corner of the social media universe.

8 Your Photoblog

The iPhone camera gets a real workout, recording moments from your trip to Tahoe, your backyard barbeque, and maybe even those offbeat, random details from your morning rush to the subway. With the iPhone camera, taking photos isn't reserved just for special occasions; it's a daily (or almost-daily) activity. Your iPhone photos are a record of what you see, what you experience, and what compels your attention. And there's no better way to publish them online than with a photoblog.

Photoblogs have been around for years; they're an early offshoot of a craze that's now crowded with cupcake blogs, sketch blogs, and blogs of every other subculture you can imagine. Like other blogs, photoblogs present their contents in a series of posts, typically organized in reverse chronological order. Sometimes the images have captions, and sometimes not; the blog form is flexible, and you can tailor it to what you would like to present. You want to dispense your photographic wisdom along with your images? No problem. You're looking to post an image a day as an experiment in photographic discipline? Go for it. Your blog is an expression of your personality, of your creativity, and of who you are. Have fun with it.

If you're hesitant, thinking you need to be an uber-techie to set up a photoblog, rest assured: Blogging has never been easier. It is now possible to set up a blog just by sending an email. That's right: You zip off an email, and you've got a blog. Want to post an image? Just email it. In fact, it's even possible to post entire slide shows just by emailing the photos to a special email address set up for your blog; seconds later, the slide show appears, formatted with a snazzy look. You'll never even glimpse a snippet of HTML or PHP code, and your blog will look awesome.

As an iPhone photographer, you're at a particular advantage when it comes to photoblogging. With a traditional camera, the photoblogging process can be a cumbersome one. To post to your blog, you have to connect a cable to your computer, transfer your images, select the ones for your blog, and then use a web-based blogging tool to post them online. (I'm exhausted just writing about this.) With the iPhone, photoblogging is an entirely different experience, because you'll be able to snap a photo and post it to your blog, within seconds, straight from your phone. The process varies depending on the blogging tool you use, but you'll typically just open a blogging app, select an image from your Camera Roll, add a caption (if you want), and tap a post button. I have taken photos, tweaked them, and posted them to my photoblog, all within a minute or two, and I've done this on train rides, hikes, and walking along the streets of New York City.

Deciding on a Look for Your Photoblog

Before you start building your photoblog, give some thought to its layout. In blogging terminology, this is often referred to as the blog's *theme*—essentially a prefab look you'll choose when you're setting up your blog. For photoblogs, you will likely want to go with one of these approaches:

▶ **Traditional**   Planning to intersperse your images with an occasional bit of verbiage? Maybe you want to describe your travels, rave about your favorite iPhone photo apps, or describe your kid's soccer game. In that case, choose a look that's adept at mixing your photos with your literary forays.

▶ **Minimalist**   If there's a classic look for photoblogs, this is it—a home page displaying just one big image. That's a dramatic way to put the emphasis on the photography and to convey that this isn't a garden-variety blog but a photoblog. If you want to spotlight your photography and you're not interested in writing text, then this is often a smart choice for a photoblog.

▶ **Series of images**   Maybe you don't like the idea of having the spotlight on a single image. If that's the case, you'll want a look that's appropriate for showcasing a series of images (see Figure 8-1). Blogging tools let you choose how many posts appear on your home page, meaning you'll get to decide whether you want to display 3 of your images, let's say, or 10 of them.

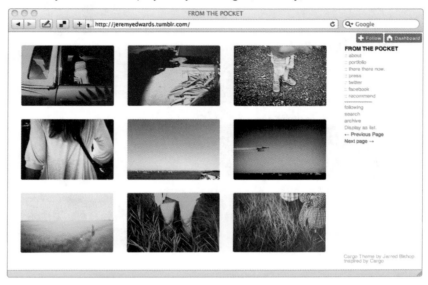

FIGURE 8-1: *Consider what sort of look you want for your photoblog.*

And what if you change your mind? No problem (or not much of one). When you get tired of one approach, simply choose another theme, and your images and your text will magically appear with the new look.

Blogging Tools

Photoblogging wasn't always as easy as it is now. Way back when, you needed to know how to install your own software on a web server running MySQL and PHP to have a slick-looking photoblog. No more. Now you have a number of choices for photoblogging, many of them essentially maintenance-free, meaning you'll never have to install or update software or have an iota of knowledge of web servers. Even better, the popular blogging tools have iPhone apps to allow you to post straight from your phone.

In this chapter, we will focus on using Tumblr for photoblogging (see Figure 8-2). Why Tumblr? For these reasons:

▶   **Simplicity**   When it comes to blogging, Tumblr is as easy as it gets.

▶   **Photo posts**   Tumblr includes a ready-made type of post just for images.

▶   **iPhone app**   The Tumblr iPhone app makes it extremely easy to post photos.

FIGURE 8-2: *A photoblog created with Tumblr, as well as the archive page displaying recent posts from a Tumblr photoblog*

▶ **Themes**   Tumblr has a variety of free (or inexpensive) themes appropriate for photoblogs. They look great.

▶ **Flexibility**   You don't need in-depth technical knowledge to alter your theme. Then again, if you know a bit of HTML/CSS, you can use your know-how to enhance your Tumblr blog—or even build your own theme.

Tumblr does a terrific job of providing a readable, fun-to-view version of your blog for viewing on the iPhone. You don't even have to choose a special mobile theme; Tumblr will reformat your blog automatically, as shown in Figure 8-3.

That's not to say you have to use Tumblr, and I also provide tips and advice for Blogger, Posterous, and WordPress—all excellent options with their own advantages. WordPress, in particular, is an amazingly versatile, always-improving choice (and open source, too). And there's one reason, in particular, you might choose one of those options over Tumblr: You know it already. If you're familiar with a blogging platform and like what it offers, go for it.

FIGURE 8-3: *A Tumblr blog, as viewed on the iPhone*

Photoblogging with Tumblr

Tumblr has millions of fans, and I'm one of them. I love Tumblr for lots of reasons, but there's one that's particularly germane to this discussion: Tumblr is wonderfully easy to learn, and you can have your blog up and running within minutes. Devote an hour or so to setting up your blog and customizing it, and you'll have a slick-looking photoblog ready for posting images from your iPhone.

＊ **NOTE: Is Tumblr a service for publishing traditional blogs or something else? The company is often viewed as being part of a trend known as *microblogging* (or *light blogging*), with the emphasis on posting brief snippets of content found online, such as quotes, photos, illustrations, and audio clips. And there's no doubt, Tumblr's suitable for that. But there's nothing "light" about Tumblr, really, other than its intuitive interface. You can use it to build a full-fledged blog or photoblog with your own original content.**

Getting Started with Tumblr

Want a Tumblr blog? Then you need a Tumblr account. Head to *http://www.tumblr .com/*, hand over your email address, and decide on a URL, with the form *http:// yourname.tumblr.com/.* If you want, you'll be able to use your own domain name for your photoblog (as explained later in the chapter).

After you sign up, you're delivered directly to your blog's Dashboard—essentially a control panel where you're able to adjust your blog's settings and post to your blog (see Figure 8-4). Since this is your virgin visit, Tumblr urges you to "Create your first post!" You can skip this for now—unless, that is, you already have a pressing item you want to post—in order to explore the Tumblr way. Tumblr has seven ready-made post types:

▶ Text	▶ Chat
▶ Photo	▶ Audio
▶ Quote	▶ Video
▶ Link	

These mean just what they say, and each has its own specialized form and a look tailored to the type of post (as shown in Figure 8-5). You can explore these forms all you want—they're entirely self-explanatory—but you know what? You may find yourself accessing them infrequently. Why's that? Because you're not creating just any type of blog. You're creating a photoblog, and it's a special type of photoblog, too—an iPhone photoblog. That means you'll be doing your posting the easiest and quickest way out there, right from your iPhone.

But there are some things you'll likely want to do from the Web, such as deciding on the look of your blog, describing what it is, and customizing it. Once you complete those tasks, you'll be ready to download the Tumblr iPhone app and start posting photos from your phone.

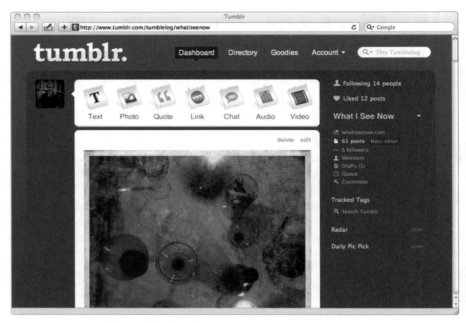

FIGURE 8-4: *Tumblr's Dashboard*

FIGURE 8-5: *The Tumblr form for posting photos via the Web*

Setting Up Your Blog

After you sign up for your blog, Tumblr provides a series of screens to complete the setup of your blog. Opt out of these, because you'll be better off familiarizing yourself with Tumblr's options without all the hand-holding from Tumblr—a smart way to get to know these in case you want to change things later. To begin setting up your blog, follow these steps from the web browser on your computer:

1. From the Tumblr Dashboard, select **Account ▸ Preferences**. Review your details to make sure everything is kosher.
2. From the Preferences page, click the **Customize your blog** button. You can also choose Customize from your Dashboard, which is in the right column.
3. Select **Info**, as shown in Figure 8-6, and then use the form provided to insert a title and description for your blog and to upload a portrait photo.
4. Next, select the **Theme** tab, which will present both paid themes and, if you scroll down, free ones. The theme determines the look of your blog, and you can't really go wrong with Tumblr's themes, because they handle photos with style. In any case, Tumblr makes it easy to change your theme at any time.
5. Click **Save**.

FIGURE 8-6: *Use the Info tab to enter a title and description for your blog and to upload a portrait photo.*

You can stop there and go straight to posting by choosing **Save + Close**, or you can make these changes, too:

▶ **Facebook and Twitter** By choosing the Services tab (see Figure 8-7), you're able to connect your Tumblr blog to your Twitter and Facebook accounts. When you post to Tumblr, your messages will automatically be posted to Twitter and shared in your Facebook news feed.

▶ **Post Count** By selecting the Advanced tab (see Figure 8-8), you're able to decide how many posts to display on your Tumblr pages. For a photoblog, you might

FIGURE 8-7: *The Services tab lets you connect your Tumblr blog to your Facebook and Twitter accounts.*

want just 3 posts, say, rather than the default, which is 10.

▶ **High-resolution photos**   Also on the Advanced tab, you can decide whether you want visitors to be able to view a high-resolution version of your photos.

Be sure to click **Save + Close** after you have made your changes. You can always alter these settings later.

Posting to Tumblr

When you post to Tumblr, you need to decide what type of post it is—a photo, a quotation, text, or one of the other options. Choose Photo, and you'll be able to upload a photo and, if you like, enter a caption. Choose Quote, and you'll be asked to enter the text of the quote and its source. Tumblr will then format your post accordingly, depending on what type of post it is.

Let's try writing a text post:

FIGURE 8-8: You can alter the number of posts per page with the Advanced tab.

1.   From your Dashboard, click the **Text** icon.
2.   Type in a title for your post. Can't think of anything? Typing **Welcome to my photoblog** will do for now.
3.   Now write a message welcoming people to your soon-to-be photoblog.
4.   Select **Create Post**.

As Figure 8-9 shows, you also have the option to add tags, view a preview of your post, and decide whether you want to publish your post now, save it as a draft, or publish it at a later date.

Using the Tumblr iPhone App

You can grab the Tumblr app (Tumblr; free) by visiting the App Store and searching for *Tumblr*. After you download the app, you will need to enter your Tumblr user name; Tumblr will then validate your account. To post a photo, follow these steps:

1.   From the bottom of the app, tap **Post**.
2.   You will see a screen with the post types—the same ones you see on the Web, as shown in Figure 8-10. Tap **Photo**.
3.   From the options (see Figure 8-11), select **Choose existing photo**. You will now be able to select an image from your Camera Roll or any of your other albums. This means you can post images you have edited with any of your iPhone photography apps and stored in your Camera Roll.

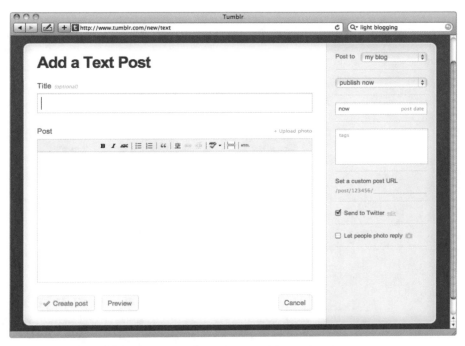

FIGURE 8-9: Tumblr's text-entry form keeps things simple.

FIGURE 8-10: You're able to choose what type of content to post from the Tumblr app.

FIGURE 8-11: Tumblr gives you several options for posting images.

4. Enter a caption, as shown in Figure 8-12. The start of your description will be used in the URL for your post; any description is better than none, because the description will help search engines index your image.
5. Choose **Open advanced options** to decide what blog to post to (if you have more than one Tumblr blog), to decide when to publish your post, and to add any tags (see Figure 8-13).
6. Tap the blue **Post** button.

FIGURE 8-12: *Writing a description or caption for a photo*

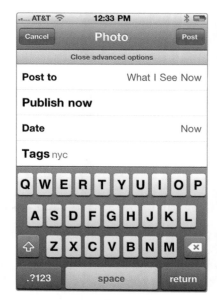

FIGURE 8-13: *Advanced options for posting*

Within moments, your photo will be live on your blog. You've done it—you've created a photoblog post right from your phone.

Customizing Your Blog

You can go a lot further in customizing your blog with Tumblr. As a start, you may want to use a web address of your own choosing—your own domain name—rather than the one Tumblr provides. Here's how:

1. Purchase a domain name from a registrar, such as GoDaddy, Namecheap, or Register.com.
2. After you have your name, follow your registrar's instructions for pointing your domain's A record to 72.32.231.8; these instructions vary from one registrar to another.
3. At Tumblr, choose Customize from your Dashboard. Select the Info tab, check the **Use a custom domain name** box, and enter the name of your domain. It can take as long as 72 hours for the changes to take effect.

Also consider these changes, accessed via the Customize screen:

▶ **Add comments with Disqus**   You can have comments for your blog by signing up for a free account with Disqus (at *http://www.disqus.com/*), a pro-vider of commenting systems for blogs and other websites. After signing up at Disqus, you will need to enter a special Disqus code, called the Disqus shortcode, at Tumblr; you will typically enter the code from the Appearance tab (from your customization options), but if there's no spot to enter it, visit *http://disqus.com/comments/ tumblr/* for instructions on entering the information elsewhere.

▶ **Accept user submissions** Interested in having others sub-mit photos to your photoblog? Then select the Community tab (as shown in Figure 8-14), provide submission guidelines, and choose what type of posts you would like others to be able to submit.

FIGURE 8-14: *Choose the Com-munity tab to allow visitors to your site to submit photos or other content.*

Exploring the Tumblr Community

At Tumblr, you'll be part of a whole community of creative types with Tumblr blogs. Check out other photographers at Tumblr by visiting *http://www.tumblr.com/ directory/photographers/*. (Select the Directory tab at Tumblr to explore other interests.) To explore the Tumblr community and meet others with similar interests, you can use Tumblr's built-in social networking tools, as shown in Figure 8-15:

▶ **Following**   If you want to keep tabs on another Tumblr site, select its Follow button—all Tumblr blogs have this button at the upper-right corner of the screen. This blog will then appear in a stream on your Dashboard. You can always unfollow someone, too.

FIGURE 8-15: *Tumblr's social networking tools get a lot of traction from Tumblr users.*

▶ **Reblogging**   See a post you just really love? Then you can reblog it—a way to have it appear on your blog, too. You can choose Reblog either from the post page or, if you're following the blogger, from the post in your Dashboard.

▶ **Liking**   From the post page, you can click a heart icon to indicate that you like a post. Some themes display your recent "likes."

Using WordPress for Your iPhone Photoblog

WordPress is now a venerable, much-loved mainstay of the media and technology worlds—an open source blogging platform widely in use as a full-fledged content management system. Homegrown bloggers use WordPress, but so do big organizations with a gazillion readers, including Ben & Jerry's, NASA, *The New York Times*, and *Rolling Stone*. It is a marvelous tool, and if you have big plans for your blog—if you're thinking it might be more like a photography magazine, say, than a photoblog—then you should explore WordPress as an option. It's remarkably flexible in its capabilities and customization options, with a vibrant community of coders and consultants available to help you develop your WordPress website.

Before you make your choice, be aware that using WordPress typically means one of two things:

▶ **You install and manage WordPress with your own hosting company.** This is the traditional way to use WordPress, where you download the software from *http://www.wordpress.org/* and then grapple with a hosted web server, a MySQL database, and other technology most photographers don't want to touch. But if you do—and it's not that difficult, if you're technically inclined—then you'll have maximum flexibility in choosing a theme for your blog and installing add-ons (known as *plug-ins*).

▶ **You sign up for a blog at WordPress.com.** Automattic, a for-profit company run by some of the people behind the WordPress software, offers free, hosted WordPress blogs at WordPress.com. With a blog at WordPress.com, you don't need to worry about installing or updating WordPress. You sign up, and you'll have your blog moments later. For an ad-free blog and to use your own domain name, you'll need to pay for premium features.

So, which is it? If you've never heard of MySQL and the idea of learning about it is terrifying, then opt for WordPress.com (or another blogging platform). Installing WordPress is relatively easy, as those things go, but it's definitely not for nontechnical neophytes.

Still not sure if it's for you? Then experiment with it. Sign up for a free WordPress.com account, download the WordPress app (Automattic; free)—a full-featured tool for posting to your blog and managing it (see Figure 8-16)—and try a few posts. Soon enough, you'll get a sense of whether you're a would-be WordPress devotee or you'd rather have something more streamlined and simple.

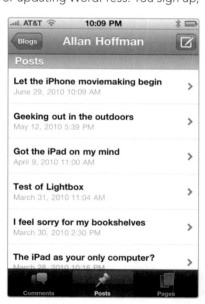

FIGURE 8-16: The WordPress app for the iPhone

Using Posterous for Your iPhone Photoblog

Posterous may have the easiest sign-up for a blog—for any online service, really—you've ever encountered. Just send an email, even one with a photo, to *post@posterous.com*, and Posterous will create your blog, post the message to your blog, and reply to you with an email about your new blog. From there, you're able to set a password for your account, upload a profile photo, revise the URL for your blog (in the form *http://yourname.posterous.com/*), use your own domain name, and otherwise start to customize your blog (see Figure 8-17). Sound familiar? Yes, Posterous is a lot like Tumblr, with many of the same features. Given how easy it is to try Posterous (and Tumblr, too), you might consider giving both a workout. The choice is largely a matter of personal preference—though Tumblr has a real edge in the way its fans use its social-networking features (such as reblogging and liking other users' posts).

Consider these factors, as well, in making your choice:

▶ **Image galleries** With Posterous, you can get awesome-looking image galleries by emailing a series of photos to Posterous.

▶ **The Posterous iPhone app** This is an app with photography at the forefront, as its name indicates: PicPosterous (Posterous; free), as shown in Figure 8-18. The app is really all about posting images—in particular, photo galleries—from your phone. If you're into text posts, you'll need to post those by email from your phone.

FIGURE 8-17: *Will Hindson's photoblog (http://willhindson.posterous.com/) runs on Posterous.*

FIGURE 8-18: *The Posterous app for the iPhone*

Using Blogger for Your iPhone Photoblog

You would think Blogger might have cornered the market on easy-to-run blogs, given its head start—Blogger was founded in 1999—and the company's subsequent acquisition by Google. No such luck. There's plenty of competition in the blogging world, and though Blogger remains popular, other companies, such as Tumblr, have gained an edge in terms of innovation and ease of use. Still, Blogger remains a relatively quick way to get started with a blog, and if you're a diehard devotee of everything Google, from Google Docs to Google Voice, then you might want to give Blogger a whirl. Keep the following in mind:

▶ **Using Blogger from your iPhone**
There's no official iPhone app for posting to Blogger. The solution? You use a third-party app to post to your blog. BlogPress (CoolLittleThings; $2.99) is a feature-laden tool for posting to Blogger and other blogging platforms (see Figure 8-19). The app handles photos quite well, even letting you decide whether you want your images hosted by Picasa Web Albums, Flickr, or BlogPress's own servers.

▶ **Beware your quota**   Images uploaded to Blogger from the Blogger website are actually stored at Picasa Web Albums, which provides 1 GB of free storage. If you're already using Picasa Web Albums for other photos, you might bump up against your storage quota.

FIGURE 8-19: The BlogPress app for the iPhone

▶ **Email your posts**   With a feature called Mail to Blogger, you can send an image to your blog to have it posted—a quick option when you don't want to fire up BlogPress from your iPhone. Just drop the photo in the email; the subject of the message will serve as the title of the post. To ensure your email signature isn't included in the post, insert **#end** after your image. You will need to set up Mail to Blogger by visiting the Settings option for your blog. Under Settings, choose Email & Mobile to configure a special email address for your posts.

Seven Tips to Get People Looking at Your Photoblog

Your photoblog may be its own reward—a visual testament to your growth as a photographer, your interests and observations, your travels, and even your opinions about iPhone photography apps, the latest photographic technology, or pretty much anything else you want to say or post. But if you go to the trouble of creating a blog and you also do an admirable job of posting photos periodically (rather than letting the blog languish, as sometimes happens), then you're likely to want to encourage other people to take a look at it. And "other people," in this context, doesn't mean just your dad and your buddies and your in-laws and their neighbors. This is the Internet, darn it, and a worldwide audience—billions of individuals with eyes peering at computer screens and cell phones and tablet computers and whatnot—awaits you.

Doesn't it? Hm. Not really. Just because you create a blog doesn't mean anyone will visit it—even if you have terrific images with witty captions. Building an audience requires work.

Here are seven ways to draw in readers and keep them happy:

▶ **Write captions**   The Web loves words. Yes, videos are popular online, and photos are, too, but there's nothing like words to attract visitors from search engines, as any expert in search engine optimization (SEO) will tell you. Describe your shots. Don't just say "Big tree." Say "Tabebuia impetiginosa, also known as the Pink trumpet tree, from a visit to the Los Angeles County Arboretum and Botanic Garden. I edited this in Photogene, toning down the color temperature and applying a custom frame." Search engines pick up those words, and visitors will follow them.

▶ **Share your know-how**   You may not think of yourself as an expert, but trust me, others can learn things from you, and they'll appreciate it. Explain why you love (or loathe) a particular iPhone photography app. Describe how you achieved a certain effect with an image. Tutorials, in particular, will help you build an audience. These don't have to be lengthy affairs. A short paragraph outlining the steps required to tweak an image can be helpful.

▶ **Title your posts**   Search engines use the titles of posts as a clue to their content. In general, be informative with your titles, rather than witty or cute. "3 steps to add a dreamy blur to your portraits" is better than "Portraits in Pixels," which doesn't really say anything.

▶ **Twitter and Facebook**   Set up your photoblog to post automatically to your social media accounts, and you'll likely gain traffic just by posting. If you're into Twitter, then retweet iPhone photos and iPhoneography tips you find online, including the photographer's Twitter address (as in *@whatiseenow*) and the hash tag *#iphoneography*, as shown in Figure 8-20.

- **Link to your blog**   Got a website? A LinkedIn profile? Then be sure to include links to your photoblog.

- **Comment**   Visit other photoblogs and comment on what you see—if, that is, you find it compelling and have something to say about it. You'll be getting your name out there, and others will likely want to check out your own photoblog.

- **Mention (or showcase) others' images**   Be generous in praising others' iPhone photos. Include a blogroll at your photoblog—a list of iPhone photographers, with links to them. If there's a photographer whose work you really love, ask for permission to post several of her images at your own blog.

FIGURE 8-20: *Twitter's #iphoneography tag*

Don't beat yourself over the head if you don't have time for all of this. Do what you can: After all, unless you have a social media assistant, these tasks could wipe out all of your leisure hours (and leave little time for actually taking photos). Focus on what you enjoy, whether it's explaining your iPhoneography techniques or developing a following on Twitter. You may not get a lot of traction just by writing one gem of a caption, but over time, as you continue to post to your blog, which is essential, you'll find more and more people viewing your iPhone photography.

9 For Inspiration

Why would professional photographers, with all of their equipment and expertise, opt to use the iPhone camera? Is it just about convenience, or is there more to it? After all, using the iPhone camera means giving up so many of the tools used by the pros: manual controls for the aperture and shutter speed, interchangeable lenses, and more. And yet even with those limitations, professional photographers have come to view the iPhone as a liberating tool for photographic creativity and experimentation. It's always with you, it provides instant gratification, and you can blast into the photographic past with a wildly innovative coterie of apps intended to bring back darkroom processes, obsolete films, and a host of tools and techniques from the era of film. What's more, you don't need to carry a boatload of equipment or hire an assistant or two when you're working with your iPhone. Sound familiar? Yes, professionals love the iPhone camera for many of the same reasons others love it.

A deserted bus stop, a kid careening down the street on his skateboard, a barren tree silhouetted by the sky—all of this, and so much more, can be material when you have a camera handy right in your pocket. There's nothing new about photographers finding inspiration in the world around them, but iPhone photography enthusiasts are taking this to another level by using their iPhone cameras, in tandem with a virtual camera bag of apps, to test the boundaries of photographic creativity. The following gallery of iPhone photography demonstrates the possibilities of iPhoneography from an international mix of photographers whose works have been exhibited in New York, Madrid, and other cities around the world.

Peter Belanger

Peter Belanger is a San Francisco–based photographer with an eclectic body of work and a love for Apple technology. His corporate clients include big players in the entertainment, media, and technology worlds, including Adobe, *Dwell* magazine, Hewlett-Packard, Pixar, Sony, and Sun. For Apple, he has photographed iPads, iPods, and other i-gadgets for product launches, and his work frequently appears in *Macworld* magazine. Needless to say, he has a lot of photographic equipment, and yet he loves his iPhone camera. In fact, he loves it so much, he used the iPhone 4 camera to photograph an iPhone 4—yes, one iPhone taking an image of another one—for a cover of *Macworld*. (He usually uses a 60-megapixel camera to shoot covers for *Macworld*.) The elaborate production is described in detail at his blog (at *http://peterbelanger.com/blog*), where he explains how he used the PhotoForge app to remove a green cast from the image and the Resize-Photo app (iLegend-Soft; $0.99) to increase the dots per inch (DPI) to meet printing requirements. After all, "What better way to showcase the phone's new camera than to have an iPhone take the photo of the iPhone on the cover?"

So what's the attraction of iPhone photography for a photographer with a national reputation and a spacious studio in San Francisco? We asked him.

Taken with an iPhone 3GS, edited with Hipstamatic (PHOTO CREDIT: Peter Belanger)

You're a pro with a 60-megapixel camera and a sophisticated studio. What's the appeal of iPhone photography?

For me, the appeal of the iPhone photography is in the many effects offered by various apps. The built-in camera may take decent images (especially the 5-megapixel camera on the iPhone 4), but I really enjoy seeing how an "unexciting" image can look so much more appealing after running it through a photo app like Picture-Show or Hipstamatic. There is a big trend right now with photographers using older equipment and embracing dated looks of specific cameras and techniques. My iPhone has been able to replicate the thrill of my old Polaroid camera. When I'm in my studio, I can even take the experience a step further using Epson's print app. The images are sent straight from my phone and pop out of the printer—instant gratification! Other times the effects are so random and unexpectedly beautiful that I try to emulate them while shooting with my Canon.

> **My iPhone has been able to replicate the thrill of my old Polaroid camera.**

Are the apps something of a blast from the photographic past?

The apps seem to rekindle a certain appeal of the processing technique as a layer of interest and aesthetic. Digital photos don't have the same "happy accidents" that one would get from film processing or from certain types of cameras. Of course, images can be altered digitally after they are shot, but it is a fun change of pace to put an image through an app and see what comes out the other end. It may be a more whimsical kind of approach, but I've seen people shooting some really stunning images with their phones, thanks to the apps.

Taken with an iPhone 3GS, edited with PictureShow
(PHOTO CREDIT: Peter Belanger)

What are three or four of your favorite apps?

My favorite photo apps are always changing, of course. Right now my top app is PictureShow. I like how it has many options to suit whatever my photo taste is at that moment. The second on the list would be SwankoLab. I appreciate that I can use an image from the Camera Roll and don't have to shoot it from within the app (like some other apps require). The third choice would be Camera+ because the split touch exposure and focus are pure genius. My fourth pick would be Epson's print app. I have the Epson Artisan 800 printer in my studio. It is an all-in-one office printer that has two paper trays. I place basic laser paper in one tray for typical office work and a stack of 4×6 glossy photo paper in the other tray. I can easily send an image from my phone to the printer without having to get the right supplies set up. It is so simple and gratifying that my iPhone practically becomes a Polaroid.

Do you have any tips for iPhoneographers?

I would encourage people to take lots of photos and not to get stuck on one app. I'm always scouring the App Store to see what new, cool photo apps I can try.

Taken with an iPhone 3GS, edited with Camera+
(PHOTO CREDIT: Peter Belanger)

Jeremy Edwards

Chicago-based photographer Jeremy Edwards says he was "immediately struck with the experience of capturing images with raw spontaneity" after buying his first iPhone and experimenting with its camera.

- ► **Web** *http://www.edwardsjeremy.com/*
- ► **Tumblr** *http://jeremyedwards.tumblr.com/*
- ► **Favorite Apps** Cross Process, Mill Colour, Photoshop Express, SwankoLab

"surf." Taken with an iPhone 3GS, edited with Cross Process and Mill Colour (PHOTO CREDIT: Jeremy Edwards)

"two piece." Taken with an iPhone 3GS, edited with Cross Process and Mill Colour (PHOTO CREDIT: Jeremy Edwards)

"ink on shoulder." Taken with an iPhone 3GS, edited with Cross Process, Mill Colour, and Photoshop Express (PHOTO CREDIT: Jeremy Edwards)

"this is them." Taken with an iPhone 3GS, edited with Photoshop Express and Lo-Mob (PHOTO CREDIT: Jeremy Edwards)

Gus Gusbano

Gus Gusbano is an Italian cameraman who likes experimenting with the endless possibilities of photography.

- ▶ **Flickr** *http://www.flickr.com/photos/gusbano/*

- ▶ **Tumblr** *http://gusbano.tumblr.com/*

- ▶ **Favorite Apps**
  SwankoLab, Photo fx, Lo-Mob, myFilm, Cross Process, BlurFX, iDOF, TiltShift Generator, Light, Pure Carbon, Cropulator, Mill Colour

"Backyard Soccer." Taken with an iPhone 2G, edited with Hipstamatic, Cool fx, Cropulator, Pure Carbon, and Photoshop Express (PHOTO CREDIT: Gus Gusbano)

"Fighting against the sun." Taken with an iPhone 2G, edited with BlurFX, TiltShift Generator, SwankoLab, Light, and Photo-Forge (PHOTO CREDIT: Gus Gusbano)

"Catwalk." Taken with an iPhone 2G, edited with myFilm, Perfectly Clear, NoiseBlaster, and Mill Colour (PHOTO CREDIT: Gus Gusbano)

Stephanie Chappe

Photography has been a big part of Stephanie Chappe's life for years, and now, with the iPhone, she has a way to share images with family, friends, and others from across the globe. "I am more connected with the subjects and scenes I am capturing, as well as the larger phone photography community from all over the world, which is a constant source of inspiration to me," she says.

▶ **Flickr** *http://www.flickr.com/photos/stephieseye/*

▶ **Web** *http://www.stephaniechappe.com/*

▶ **Favorite App** Photogene

"Portrait." Taken with an iPhone 3G, edited with Hipstamatic and Photogene (PHOTO CREDIT: Stephanie Chappe)

"I like puddles." Taken with an iPhone 3GS, edited with Photo fx, Photogene, and TiltShift Generator (PHOTO CREDIT: Stephanie Chappe)

"Curious." Taken with an iPhone 3G, edited with TiltShift Generator (PHOTO CREDIT: Stephanie Chappe)

Tony Cece

Video producer and humanitarian photographer Tony Cece captures images of an astonishing variety of subjects, from seemingly mundane glimpses of beauty to stark visions of poverty.

▶ **Flickr** *http://www.flickr.com/photos/iphonelomo/*

▶ **Web** *http://www.iphonelomo.com/*

▶ **Favorite Apps** Photo fx, Vignetting Lens, TiltShift Generator, Photogene, PictureShow, Hipstamatic, CameraBag, AutoStitch, Flickit

"Streets of India." Taken with an iPhone 3GS, edited with Hipstamatic (PHOTO CREDIT: Tony Cece)

"Shop Tree Beauty." Taken with an iPhone 3GS, edited with Hipstamatic (PHOTO CREDIT: Tony Cece)

"The Birds." Taken with an iPhone 3GS, edited with CameraBag, Photo fx, Cool fx, and Photogene (PHOTO CREDIT: Tony Cece)

"Egypt." Taken with an iPhone 3GS, edited with Lofi (PHOTO CREDIT: Tony Cece)

MissPixels

MissPixels, as she likes to be called, is a graphic designer and artistic director who captures "pictorial accidents." She considers the iPhone "a symbolic extension of my arm, my hand—a new type of brush."

- ▶ **Web** *http://www.misspixels.com/*
- ▶ **Flickr** *http://www.flickr.com/photos/misspixels/*
- ▶ **Favorite Apps** Photoshop Express, TiltShift Generator, PhotoForge, CameraBag, PictureShow

I love the opportunity to take pictures discreetly, without people noticing me. With a traditional camera, people are more impressed and less natural. The iPhone allows me to capture very natural moments, like a quick glance.

"Born to be Wild." Taken with an iPhone 3GS, edited with Photoshop Express, TiltShift Generator, and CameraBag (PHOTO CREDIT: MissPixels)

"Eat Me." Taken with an iPhone 3GS, edited with Photoshop Express and Spica (PHOTO CREDIT: MissPixels)

"4th of July." Taken with an iPhone 3GS, edited with PhotoForge, Photoshop Express, and Picture-Show (PHOTO CREDIT: MissPixels)

(Not Just) for Photo Professionals

For professional photographers, the iPhone is far more than a camera. It is, for many photographers, an essential element of their photographic tool kit, integrated into their work processes and useful for a variety of tasks beyond making phone calls to clients and maintaining a contacts list. With the iPhone, photographers are able to calculate exposure and depth of field for digital SLRs (dSLRs), fire off the shutter on their dSLRs (with the iPhone as a remote), and have models sign releases (yes, right on the phone, with a finger as a substitute for ink). Even if you're not a pro, you may find some of the apps favored by the pros useful when you're using a camera other than your iPhone.

▶ **DSLR Camera Remote Professional Edition (onOne Software; $19.99)** Connect your Canon or Nikon SLR to a computer with a Wi-Fi connection, and you can fire off shots, adjust camera settings, and review images right from your iPhone.

▶ **f/8 DoF Calculator (Bitwerkz; $3.99)** Use the app in tandem with your camera—your other camera, that is, and not your iPhone camera—to calculate depth of field and determine what will be in focus (and blurred) in your images.

▶ **Focalware (Spiral Development; $4.99)** Wondering whether your far-off location for a photo shoot will have the right light at the right time? This app tells you the position of the sun and moon for any location and date.

▶ **PlaceTagger (return7; $9.99)** Use this app to help you tag your non-iPhone photos with precise geographical data.

▶ **Easy Release (ApplicationGap; $9.99)** Have the subjects of your images review your custom model release form and sign it, right on the iPhone. Easy Release generates PDFs for clients and your own records.

The iPhoneography Community

Looking to get inspired by the work of other iPhone photographers? The iPhoneography community is thriving at photoblogs, Flickr, and even "real-world" art galleries. Look to the following spots for inspiration:

▸ **Flickr** Join Flickr (see Chapter 7), and you can connect with iPhone photographers in groups devoted to every aspect of iPhone photography, from general iPhoneography (see *http://www.flickr.com/groups/iphoneography/*) to the Hipstamatic app (see *http://www.flickr.com/groups/hipstamatic/*).

▸ **Tumblr** By "liking" other people's images, following other photographers, and commenting on what you see, you can develop your own community of iPhone photography enthusiasts at Tumblr (see Chapter 8).

▸ **iPhoneography Blogs** For the latest on iPhone photography news, reviews of apps, and stories about iPhone photographers, visit iPhoneogenic (at *http://iphoneogenic.tumblr.com/*), iPhoneography (at *http://www.iphoneography.com/*), and Life in Lofi (at *http://www.lifeinlofi.com/*).

▸ **Community Apps** A number of apps allow you to produce eye-popping effects and also contribute your images to lively photo communities. These include Best Camera (Ubermind; $2.99), Instagram (Burbn; free), and picplz (picplz; free).

▸ **Exhibitions and Contests** The iPhone photography blogs typically provide details about new contests and exhibitions. A number of these have gained acclaim, including EYE'EM (at *http://www.eyeem.com/*) and Pixels at an Exhibition (at *http://pixelsatanexhibition.com/*).

The iPhone photography community just keeps growing, and it's likely to expand and evolve as more and more people discover the thrill of transforming their images with the amazingly creative apps available for the iPhone.

INDEX

MY NEW™ iPAD, 2ND EDITION

A User's Guide

by WALLACE WANG

Apple's iPad has revolutionized the way consumers experience the Web, email, photos, and video. As with all Apple gadgets, the basic features are easy to access and understand. But there's a world of possibility beyond the basics, and many users need guidance to make the most of their iPads. *My New iPad* takes readers step by step through the iPad's many useful features, so you can do things like surf the Internet, send email, listen to music, take notes, read ebooks, use iWork, and play with digital photos. And since no one wants to read a long, dry textbook to learn how to use their new toy, author Wallace Wang takes a practical, easy-to-follow approach and keeps the tone light.

DECEMBER 2010, 384 PP., $24.95
ISBN 978-1-59327-287-6

MY NEW™ MAC, SNOW LEOPARD EDITION

54 Simple Projects to Get You Started

by WALLACE WANG

Mac OS X Snow Leopard is a beautiful operating system, but it can be confusing to brand-new Mac owners—especially if they come from Windows. Using 54 essential step-by-step projects every Mac owner should know, *My New Mac, Snow Leopard Edition* encourages readers to treat their new computer as an opportunity for fun and exploration, not something serious and overwhelming. Rather than focus each chapter on a specific program or feature of Snow Leopard (as most beginner books do), Wallace Wang takes a project-oriented approach that mirrors the sorts of things people want to do with their Macs, such as surf the Internet, send email, listen to CDs, take notes, or play with digital photos.

AUGUST 2009, 512 PP., $29.95
ISBN 978-1-59327-209-8

THE BOOK OF™ INKSCAPE

The Definitive Guide to the Free Graphics Editor

by DMITRY KIRSANOV

Inkscape is a powerful, free, cross-platform, vector-based drawing tool similar to Adobe Illustrator and CorelDRAW. *The Book of Inkscape*, written by Inkscape developer and graphic designer Dmitry Kirsanov, is an in-depth guide to Inkscape, offering comprehensive coverage and creative advice on Inkscape's many capabilities. Following an overview of vector-based graphics in general and SVG in particular, Kirsanov takes the reader from basic techniques—selecting, transforming, styling—to more advanced topics such as gradients and patterns, path editing, artistic drawing, clones and patterns, working with text, exporting bitmaps, and using extensions.

SEPTEMBER 2009, 480 PP., $44.95
ISBN 978-1-59327-181-7

THE MANGA GUIDE™ TO PHYSICS

by HIDEO NITTA, KEITA TAKATSU, *and* TREND-PRO CO., LTD.

The Manga Guide to Physics teaches readers the fundamentals of physics through authentic Japanese manga. Megumi, an all-star tennis player, is struggling to pass her physics class. Luckily for her, she befriends Ryota, a patient physics geek who uses real-world examples to help her understand classical mechanics. Readers follow along with Megumi as she learns about the physics of everyday objects like roller skates, slingshots, braking cars, and tennis rackets. As the book progresses, Megumi begins to master even the toughest concepts of physics, like momentum and impulse, parabolic motion, and the relationship between force, mass, and acceleration. Using a lively and quirky approach, *The Manga Guide to Physics* combines a whimsical story with real educational content so that readers will quickly master the core concepts of physics with a minimum of frustration.

MAY 2009, 248 PP., $19.95
ISBN 978-1-59327-196-1

THE MANGA GUIDE™ TO MOLECULAR BIOLOGY

by MASAHARU TAKEMURA, SAKURA, *and* BECOM CO., LTD.

The Manga Guide to Molecular Biology teaches the fundamentals of molecular biology through authentic Japanese manga. After snoozing their way through Molecular Biology 101, Ami and Rin are forced to take make-up classes. With the help of Dr. Moro and his virtual reality machine, they travel inside cells, meeting cell organelles, nuclei, and genes and chromosomes face to face. They examine proteins and amino acids, watch DNA replicate and cells divide, and meet exciting characters like Enzyme Man. Once the girls learn the fundamentals of genetics, they learn about recombinant technology, cloning, and the role of molecular biology in fighting diseases. With an engaging storyline and charming characters, *The Manga Guide to Molecular Biology* makes learning this essential discipline lively and painless.

AUGUST 2009, 240 PP., $19.95
ISBN 978-1-59327-202-9

PHONE:
800.420.7240 OR
415.863.9900
MONDAY THROUGH FRIDAY,
9 AM TO 5 PM (PST)

FAX:
415.863.9950
24 HOURS A DAY,
7 DAYS A WEEK

EMAIL:
SALES@NOSTARCH.COM

WEB:
WWW.NOSTARCH.COM

MAIL:
NO STARCH PRESS
38 RINGOLD STREET
SAN FRANCISCO, CA 94103
USA

Updates

Visit *http://www.nostarch.com/iphone_photo.htm* for updates, errata, and other information.

Create Great iPhone Photos is set in Avenir. The book was printed and bound at Friesens in Altona, Manitoba in Canada. The paper is Domtar Husky 60# Smooth, which is certified by the Forest Stewardship Council (FSC). This book uses a layflat binding, which allows it to lie flat when open.